ESSENTIAL CHEMISTRY

ACIDS AND BASES

ESSENTIAL CHEMISTRY

ESSENTIAL CHEMISTRY

ACIDS AND BASES

KRISTI LEW

CHELSEA HOUSE
PUBLISHERS
An imprint of Infobase Publishing

ACIDS AND BASES

Chelsea House
An imprint of Infobase Publishing
132 West 31st Street
New York NY 10001

Library of Congress Cataloging-in-Publication Data

Lew, Kristi.
  Acids and bases / Kristi Lew.
      p. cm. — (Essential chemistry)
  Includes bibliographical references and index.
  ISBN 978-0-7910-9783-0 (hardcover)
  1. Acids. 2. Bases (Chemistry) I. Title. II. Series.

  QD477.L49 2008
  546'.24—dc22   2008024015

CONTENTS

A World of Acids and Bases

The world as we know it could not function without acids and bases. These chemical compounds are used extensively, from the chemical laboratory to the manufacturing industry. They are necessary for the proper functioning of the human body and for the health of the environment, too. Acids taste sour, break down metals, and react with bases. Without acids, soft drinks, lemonade, and tomato sauce would not taste the same way. Bases taste bitter, feel slippery, and react with acids. Without bases, cakes would be hard and flat, and laundry detergent would not clean. Both acids and bases can change certain vegetable substances a variety of different colors, and they can burn through human skin if not handled properly. Without acids and bases, we would not have dynamite, some heart medications, and fertilizers. On the other hand, without acids, we would not have damaging acid rain. And the surface of Venus would not be the uninhabitable furnace that we know it to be.

SULFURIC ACID CLOUDS OF VENUS

Earth is not the only planet in the solar system where acids are found. In fact, some planets contain acids in much greater abundance than found on Earth. For example, because of their similar size, Earth and Venus are often called twin planets. There is one very important difference, however, between the two—their atmospheres. Earth's atmosphere is made up of 79% nitrogen, 20% oxygen, and 1% other gases—just right for the survival of humans and other living things. Venus, on the other hand, is surrounded by thick clouds of carbon dioxide, nitrogen, and sulfuric acid—conditions where living things cannot survive.

Scientists believe that the sulfur in Venus' atmosphere came from volcanic eruptions. Earth has experienced its fair share of volcanic eruptions, too. However, the sulfur from early eruptions on Earth was incorporated into solid sulfur compounds. Indeed, sulfur is an important element found in many of the compounds that make up Earth's crust.

An **element** is a substance that cannot be broken down into simpler substances by ordinary chemical means. A chemical **compound** is a substance made up of two or more elements that have been chemically bonded together. Scientists believe that solid sulfur compounds do not exist on Venus like they do on Earth because, at about 900° Fahrenheit (480° Celsius), the surface temperature on Venus is too hot for them to form in the first place. This temperature is well above the melting point of sulfur (235°F [113°C]). Therefore, instead of being incorporated into rocks, the sulfur on Venus continues to float around in the atmosphere in the form of the chemical compound sulfur dioxide (SO_2).

The sulfur dioxide in Venus' atmosphere is turned into sulfuric acid by two different chemical reactions. In the first reaction, the sulfur dioxide reacts with oxygen to form sulfur trioxide:

The thick clouds surrounding the planet Venus are made up of carbon dioxide, nitrogen, and sulfuric acid. Living things cannot survive in such harsh conditions.

$$2\ SO_2 \quad + \quad O_2 \quad \rightarrow \quad 2\ SO_3$$

sulfur   oxygen   sulfur

dioxide   trioxide

The oxygen that reacts with the sulfur dioxide comes from water (H_2O) that is also present in Venus' atmosphere. When the sun's high-energy ultraviolet (UV) rays hit a water molecule, it dissociates (breaks down) into hydrogen and oxygen—the elements that make up water.

Once formed, the sulfur trioxide reacts with water vapor to form sulfuric acid:

$$SO_3 \quad + \quad H_2O \quad \rightarrow \quad H_2SO_4$$

sulfur   water   sulfuric acid

trioxide

Sulfur dioxide also exists in Earth's atmosphere. It is released by the burning of fossil fuels, such as coal and gasoline, in power plants and automobiles. Once in the atmosphere, the sulfur dioxide undergoes the same processes as it does in Venus' atmosphere to produce sulfuric acid.

The clouds around Venus contain relatively large droplets of sulfuric acid, which occasionally rain down on the surface of the planet, or at least they try to, because the temperature is so high that the droplets evaporate before they actually reach the surface. (This "almost rain" is called *virga*, the term for any kind of precipitation that evaporates before it reaches the ground.) On Earth, however, the sulfuric acid does not evaporate but falls to the ground as acid rain, an environmental pollutant that can destroy buildings and harm plants and animals.

Almost 80% of the sunlight that hits Venus is reflected back into space by the thick clouds surrounding the planet before it ever reaches the surface. Even so, temperatures at the surface of Venus are much hotter than those on Earth. However, this is not because Venus is closer to the Sun than the Earth. Scientists believe that the difference in the temperatures of the two planets is due to a runaway greenhouse effect caused by the large amount of sulfur dioxide in Venus' atmosphere.

Sulfur dioxide is a greenhouse gas, as is carbon dioxide. Both of these gases are called greenhouse gases because they trap heat very much like the glass in a greenhouse. Greenhouses are usually small structures made largely of glass. The glass allows sunlight to penetrate the greenhouse just as carbon dioxide and other greenhouse gases allow sunlight to pass through Earth's atmosphere.

The glass of a greenhouse, however, keeps the radiant energy from the Sun from escaping. This energy is changed to thermal energy, which remains trapped inside the greenhouse in the same way that the greenhouse gases of the atmosphere keep heat from escaping the Earth. In a greenhouse, this energy makes the atmosphere inside warm enough for plants to grow. On Earth, it makes the planet's average temperature 60°F (15.5°C), which is warmer than it would be otherwise. A certain amount of greenhouse gases in the atmosphere is necessary for life on Earth to thrive. Too much of a good thing, however, can lead to problems, as Venus' very efficient greenhouse-like atmosphere and high surface temperatures show.

RELIEF WITH A BANG

Sulfuric acid is not all bad. In fact, it has many useful functions. One of those is to make nitroglycerin. Nitroglycerin is needed to make explosives like dynamite, but it is also used as a medicine. This dual-purpose chemical compound was discovered by Italian chemist Ascanio Sobrero (1812–1888) in 1847.

At the time of his discovery, Sobrero was a student of French chemist Théophile-Jules Pelouze (1807–1867), who was investigating another explosive substance—guncotton. Guncotton, or nitrocellulose, was discovered in 1846 when a German chemist named Christian Friedrich Schönbein (1799–1868) poured a mixture of nitric and sulfuric acids over a wad of cotton. At first, Schönbein was less than impressed with the results of his experiment. The dry, treated cotton looked just like any other wad of cotton. Imagine Schönbein's surprise when he lit a match near the fibrous bundle and—poof! A brilliant, smokeless flame gobbled up the cotton, leaving no trace of it behind. Cotton that had not been treated with the acid mixture, on the other hand, would have left behind a pile of ash and unburned material. Schönbein had discovered a form of smokeless gunpowder.

Like guncotton, nitroglycerin is made by combining concentrated sulfuric and nitric acids. Instead of pouring the mixture over cotton, however, Sobrero mixed the acids with glycerol (also called glycerin). Glycerol is a colorless, odorless, sweet-tasting liquid. When glycerol is mixed with sulfuric and nitric acids, however, the mixture explodes.

Pure nitroglycerin is a "contact explosive." That means that any little bump or jolt can cause it to explode. This makes pure nitroglycerin extremely dangerous to handle or transport. In fact, after an explosion in the late 1840s that badly scarred Sobrero's face, he deemed nitroglycerin much too dangerous to work with. He implored all scientists to stay away from this dangerous substance. He became terribly frightened of nitroglycerin and was deeply embarrassed to have his name linked to its discovery.

Nitroglycerin not only blows up when it is mechanically shocked (dropped, hit, or jarred, for example) but also when it

CRUMBLING PAPER

Acid-free paper is all the rage for people who assemble scrapbooks as a hobby. For those who are trying to preserve sentimental objects, such as photographs, handwritten mementos, a wedding dress, or a quilt to pass down through generations of the family, acid-free paper is a necessity. The problem is that acids play a very important part in the paper manufacturing process. Most paper is made from wood. To get from wood to paper, an acid is used to break down the fibers that hold the wood together. Acid-free paper has been taken though an extra manufacturing step to remove the acid. This process makes the paper neutral or even a little basic. Slightly basic paper is called buffered paper.

Why does the amount of acid in paper make such a difference? Acids are corrosive chemicals. Corrosive chemicals can destroy material or living tissue on contact. Paper does not contain enough acid to burn skin, but over time the paper becomes stiff and brittle and eventually falls apart. As a result, precious personal memories or important historical documents that were written on acidic paper can be lost. Acid-containing paper can also transfer the acid to other objects in a process called *acid migration*. The acid can weaken or destroy the fibers in fabrics. It can also ruin photographs. Therefore, to preserve those irreplaceable memories, be sure to use paper that is acid-free.

is heated to 424°F (218°C). Its volatility, or instability, is due to the fact that it contains both a fuel and an oxidizing agent, both of which are needed for combustion (or burning) to occur. Once nitroglycerin is ignited, an **exothermic** reaction—a reaction that gives off heat—takes place. Igniting nitroglycerin gives off enough heat to keep the reaction going. The reaction also creates a lot of quickly expanding gases which, in turn, create a very large bang.

People wishing to preserve old memories on paper, such as in a scrapbook, should use acid-free paper. This is because acid can make paper brittle and fall apart over a long period of time. It can also seep into and destroy fibers in fabrics, or ruin photographs.

Nitroglycerin is a chemical compound used to make explosions such as the one at right, generated during a reenactment of an oil well being shot with a nitroglycerine torpedo. It can also, however, be used as a medicine to relieve chest pain or stop heart attacks.

In 1863, against Sobrero's wishes, Alfred Nobel (1833–1896), a Swedish chemist and fellow student of Pelouze, developed the blasting cap, a triggering mechanism that could deliver a mechanical shock to nitroglycerin and cause it to explode. In 1865, Nobel built the first nitroglycerin manufacturing factory despite losing his brother, Emil, a year earlier in an accidental explosion that occurred while Emil was preparing nitroglycerin. Nobel discovered that if the nitroglycerin was mixed with other materials, it was much less likely to explode after being jarred or dropped. Nobel finally settled on mixing the oily liquid with a porous sedimentary rock (called diatomaceous earth) to make dynamite.

Alfred Nobel's invention made blasting rock, building canals, digging tunnels, and many other construction tasks much easier. Nobel did well in the dynamite business and eventually opened 90 factories and laboratories in more than 20 countries. By the time of his death in 1896, he held 355 patents—not only for explosives, but also for developing synthetic rubber, leather, and silk. Upon his passing, Nobel left instructions that his considerable fortune be used to award an annual prize to scientists and others who have made great contributions to physics, chemistry, physiology or medicine, literature, and peace. Thus, the Nobel Prize was born.

Nitroglycerin is not only used as an explosive, however. It has another use—as a medicine. Nitroglycerin tablets are often prescribed to ease chest pain (angina) and stop heart attacks. How does taking a dose of a highly explosive substance help someone who is having a heart attack? It seems that nitroglycerin is not only helpful in blowing things up, but it is also a vasodilator. Vasodilators relax blood vessels and increase blood flow—exactly what the heart needs in the event of a heart attack or chest pain. Doctors have been prescribing nitroglycerin for chest pain since 1879. In fact, just before he died, Alfred Nobel's doctors prescribed nitroglycerin to treat his heart disease. Nobel refused to take it, not because he was afraid he would explode—the nitroglycerin used in the pills is in very small amounts that are further diluted with other inert ingredients—but because he could not stand the headaches that are a common side effect of the medication.

When doctors started prescribing nitroglycerin, they had no idea how it worked, only that it did. It was not until 1977 that an American physician and pharmacologist named Ferid Murad discovered that nitroglycerin is converted into the chemical nitric oxide in the body. In the 1980s, two other American pharmacologists, Robert Furchgott and Louis Ignarro, discovered that nitric oxide was responsible for signaling the muscles of the blood vessels to relax. In 1998, Murad, Furchgott, and Ignarro received the Nobel Prize in Medicine.

When Murad, Furchgott, and Ignarro received their Nobel Prizes, however, scientists still did not know exactly how nitroglycerin was broken down by the body and converted into nitric oxide. In 2002, researchers at Duke University in North Carolina found an enzyme in mitochondria, the cell's "powerhouse," that they believe is responsible for this process. This discovery also explained a phenomenon that doctors had long observed—over time, nitroglycerin stops working and no longer relieves the patient's chest pain.

According to the Duke University study, there is a finite amount of the enzyme that breaks down the nitroglycerin in the mitochondria. Once the enzyme is "used up," nitroglycerin no longer works for that patient.

EVERYDAY ACIDS AND BASES

These are some of the more exotic examples of acids and bases. As mentioned earlier, however, these chemicals also play important roles in everyday life. For example, orange juice, lemonade, and

GRAVE WAX

"Grave wax" is a term for a crumbly, waxy substance called *adipocere*. Adipocere starts to form on the human body about a month after it is buried. It forms easily on the fatty parts of the body such as the cheeks, abdomen, and buttocks. The waxy adipocere protects the body from further decomposition and has even been found on 100-year-old exhumed corpses. This buildup occurs when a body is buried in highly basic (alkaline) soil. The waxy substance is produced by a chemical reaction between the basic soil and fats in the body in a process called *saponification*. Saponification is also the process used in the manufacture of soap.

It takes time for adipocere to form, however, so if insects get to the body and eat the fleshy bits fairly quickly, the process is not likely to take place. But if conditions are right, adipocere can form all over the surface of a body, producing what is commonly called a "soap mummy."

Want to see a soap mummy? The Mütter Museum in Philadelphia, Pennsylvania, has one. She is called the "Soap Woman." A man who was buried next to her and who also turned into a soap mummy is sometimes displayed in the Smithsonian Institute in Washington, D.C., too. Not surprisingly, he is called the "Soap Man."

Above are some common household acids and bases. The items on the left—
vitamin C, aspirin, and vinegar—contain acids. The items on the right—milk of
magnesia, baking soda, and drain cleaner—contain bases.

soda pop would not taste the way they do if they did not contain
an acid. Orange juice and lemonade contain citric acid, which
is naturally present in all citrus fruits. Citrus fruits also contain
another acid: ascorbic acid, which is also known as vitamin C.

Colas and other sodas contain phosphoric acid, which gives
these beverages their tangy taste. Apples contain malic acid, which
gives them their tart flavor. Vinegar is a 5% solution of ethanoic
acid (also called acetic acid) and water.

Like acids, bases have many important uses. Ammonia, soap,
and other cleaners work to dissolve dirt because of their basic

ACID-WASHED JEANS

The term "acid" is sometimes used in misleading ways. Take acid-washed jeans, for example. Want to know a secret? They are not really washed with acid. Actually, these jeans are tossed into a washing machine with porous volcanic rocks that have been specially treated so that they can absorb bleach. When the jeans come into contact with the bleach-soaked rocks, the indigo dye in the denim is destroyed by the bleach. The exact type of rock used is a tightly held secret. In fact, before the jeans can leave the factory, each pocket of acid-washed jeans must be thoroughly searched to make sure a wayward rock is not left behind for competitors to find. What makes the name a little misleading is that bleach is not an acidic but actually a slightly basic solution. So, these jeans really should be called "basic-washed jeans" or "alkali-washed jeans" or even "volcanic-washed jeans"—anything but acid-washed jeans.

properties. Fertilizers are everyday substances that can be either acidic or basic. They are used to adjust the chemical composition of soil to enable the plants to grow. So people use acids and bases every day, but how can you tell if a substance is an acid or a base?

What are Acids and Bases?

Acids and bases are determined by their properties. The word acid comes from the Latin word *acidus*, which means "sour." For example, lemon juice tastes sour because it contains citric acid. Sauerkraut, another sour-tasting food, is cabbage fermented in lactic acid. In fact, *sauer* (pronounced almost exactly like the English word sour) in German means "acid." Sour cream also has lactic acid in it.

Substances can have other properties that define them as acids. For example, acids can dissolve some metals, such as lead and zinc. They change litmus (a dye made from lichens) from blue to pink, and they react with bases to form a **salt** and water.

Bases have specific properties that mark them as bases, too. Bases taste bitter, but most bases are not food, so they should not be tasted. In fact, no chemical substance should ever be tasted unless you are positive it is safe. Bases also feel slippery to

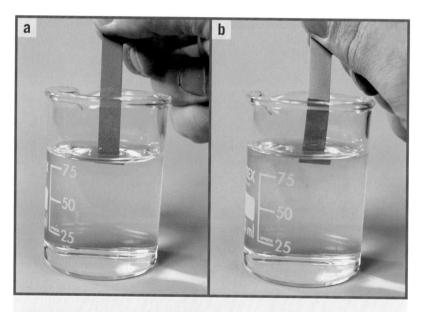

(a) Acidic solutions change litmus paper from blue to pink.
(b) Alkaline (basic) solutions change litmus paper from pink to blue.

the touch because they denature proteins. Denaturing a protein changes its shape. A change in a protein's shape may also cause a change in the way it works. It can even cause the protein to not work at all. Because humans are made up mostly of proteins, people need to be very careful around strong bases such as oven cleaners, which contain lye (sodium or potassium hydroxide), or strong acids such as sulfuric acid. Bases change pink litmus blue and react with acids to form a salt and water. Bases are also called alkalis.

Acids and bases are almost always found as aqueous solutions—that is, dissolved in water. Solutions of both acids and bases are called **electrolytes**. Electrolytes conduct **electricity,** which is the movement of electrons or other charged particles. When an acid or a base is dissolved in water, they break down into their **ions,** which are charged particles. These ions are capable of conducting an electric current, which is a stream of moving electric charges.

HISTORY OF ACID AND BASE CHEMISTRY

Robert Boyle (1627–1691), an Irish chemist, was the first person to classify certain chemicals as either acids or bases. Boyle based his classifications on their properties. He was unable to explain, however, why acids and bases have the properties that they do. It would be another 200 years before a scientist came along to answer that question. That scientist was the Swedish chemist Svante Arrhenius (1859–1927).

Arrhenius Acids and Bases

Arrhenius was the first scientist to explain that when water dissolves a substance, that substance breaks down into its ions. An ion is a charged particle that is formed when an **atom** gives up or takes on **electrons**. An atom is the smallest unit of an element that still has the properties of that element. Atoms are the building blocks of all matter.

Atoms are made up of three basic subatomic particles, one of which is an electron. The other two subatomic particles are **protons** and **neutrons**. Protons and electrons both carry an electrical charge. Protons are positively charged while electrons are negatively charged. Protons are located in the **nucleus**, or center, of an atom. Electrons move rapidly around the outside of the nucleus in a series of energy levels, or *shells*. In a neutral atom, the number of protons inside the nucleus is equal to the number of electrons moving around it. Because the atom contains an equal number of positively charged protons and negatively charged electrons, the atom's net charge is zero.

When an atom loses or gains one or more electrons, it is left with an unequal number of charges. Because the charges no longer balance out, the atom becomes a charged particle, or an ion.

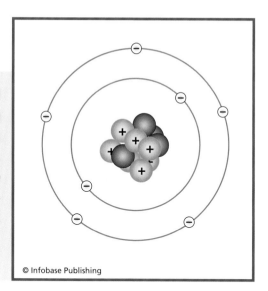

Electrons travel around the nucleus of an atom and are located in a series of energy levels, or shells, that increase in energy as their distance from the nucleus increases.

© Infobase Publishing

When an atom loses electrons, it has more positively charged protons in its nucleus than it has negatively charged electrons moving around its nucleus, giving it an overall positive charge. This creates a positive ion. When an atom loses one electron, its ion will have a charge of +1. If the atom loses two electrons, its ion has a +2 charge and so on. On the other hand, when an atom gains electrons, it now has more electrons than protons and a negative ion is formed. A positive ion is called a **cation**. An **anion** is a negatively charged ion.

Arrhenius proposed the idea that when an acid dissolves in water, it dissociates, or breaks, into its ions. This process is called **ionization** or **disassociation**. For example, the compound hydrogen chloride dissociates into a positive hydrogen ion and a negative chlorine ion when dissolved in water. This disassociation forms hydrochloric acid.

The charges of ions are designated with superscripts placed beside the symbol for the ion. For example, a hydrogen ion is abbreviated H^+. The letter "H" is the chemical symbol for hydrogen. The superscript plus sign shows that the hydrogen ion has a single positive charge. (The number one is not written, but is understood by chemists to be there.) The chlorine ion, on the other hand, is a negative ion. Therefore, it has a minus sign next to it:

$$HCl \,(aq) \quad \rightarrow \quad H^+ \,(aq) \quad + \quad Cl^- \,(aq)$$

| hydrochloric | hydrogen | chlorine |
| acid | ion | ion |

The designation (aq) indicates a water solution. (Three other chemical states and their formula notations include liquid (l), solid (s), and gas (g).) The substance is in a **solution,** which is defined as a **homogenous** mixture of two or more substances. Homogenous means that the solution has a uniform chemical makeup. In other words, if you took samples of a solution from two different areas of its container, the two samples would look the same and have the same chemical composition, as would, say, two spoonfuls of vanilla ice cream scooped from different parts of the same container. In comparison, a **heterogeneous** mixture has a different makeup in different places. A pepperoni pizza, for example, is a heterogeneous mixture. If a sample is taken from one part of the pizza, it is likely to contain a different amount of pepperoni, cheese, pizza sauce, and crust than a sample from another part of the same pizza.

Arrhenius thought something similar to disassociation happened to bases, too. But he believed that instead of releasing a positive hydrogen ion like acids do, bases contributed a hydroxide ion to the solution. A hydroxide ion is a negative ion, and it is written OH^-. For example, if the base sodium hydroxide is dissolved in water, it will break up into sodium ions and hydroxide ions, as follows:

$$NaOH \,(aq) \quad \rightarrow \quad Na^+ \,(aq) \quad + \quad OH^- \,(aq)$$

| sodium hydroxide | sodium | hydroxide |
| solution | ion | ion |

So, Arrhenius defined an acid as any substance that releases hydrogen ions (H^+) when it is dissolved in water. He defined a base as any substance that releases hydroxide ions (OH^-). This would explain why acids all have similar properties—because they all release H^+ ions. It also explains the similarities among bases. All bases, according to Arrhenius' definition, release OH^- ions. It also explains why water forms when acids and bases are mixed:.

$$H^+ \quad + \quad OH^- \quad \rightarrow \quad H_2O$$

hydrogen   hydroxide   water
    ion   ion   molecule

A hydrogen atom is composed of one proton in its nucleus and one electron in orbit around the nucleus. When a hydrogen atom loses its one electron to form the positive hydrogen ion, the only thing left behind is a proton. Therefore, hydrogen ions are sometimes called protons. Acids such as nitric acid (HNO_3) or hydrochloric acid (HCl) release only one hydrogen atom, or proton, into solution. Such acids are called monoprotic acids. Sulfuric acid (H_2SO_4), on the other hand, releases two hydrogen atoms and is, therefore, a diprotic acid. Phosphoric acid (H_3PO_4) is a triprotic acid. Any acid that releases more than one hydrogen atom (including diprotic and triprotic acids) is called a polyprotic acid.

Similarly, bases made from the metals of Group I on the periodic table, such as sodium hydroxide (NaOH) or potassium hydroxide (KOH), are called monobasic because they release one hydroxide ion into solution. Bases made up of Group II metals, such as calcium hydroxide [$Ca(OH)_2$] or magnesium hydroxide [$Mg(OH)_2$], release two hydroxide ions and are therefore dibasic. Like acids, any base that is capable of releasing more than one hydroxide ion into solution is called polybasic.

Arrhenius' theory explained a lot about acids and bases, but it did not explain everything. Not all bases release hydroxide ions. In fact, one of the most commonly used bases—baking soda

($NaHCO_3$)—does not contain any hydroxide ions. So why does it act as a base?

Brønsted-Lowry Acids and Bases

In 1923, two scientists, working independently, came up with an idea that would explain how substances that do not contain hydroxide ions could act as a base. A Danish scientist, Johannes Brønsted (1879–1947), and an English chemist named Thomas Lowry (1874–1936) both published papers about the same time stating that a base is any substance that accepts a proton (a hydrogen ion). Brønsted and Lowry's definitions explained how bases that do not contain the hydroxide ion work. Their definition also works for bases that do contain the hydroxide ion.

Recall that if hydrogen chloride (HCl) is added to water, it releases its hydrogen ions, producing hydrochloric acid. The ions present in hydrochloric acid are hydrogen ions (H^+) and chlorine ions (Cl^-):

$$HCl\ (aq) \rightarrow H^+\ (aq)\ +\ Cl^-\ (aq)$$

hydrochloric   hydrogen   chlorine

acid   ion   ion

When the base sodium hydroxide (NaOH) is dissolved in water, it also dissociates into its ions, sodium ions (Na^+) and hydroxide ions (OH^-):

$$NaOH\ (aq) \rightarrow Na^+\ (aq)\ +\ OH^-\ (aq)$$

sodium hydroxide   sodium   hydroxide

solution   ion   ion

If these two aqueous solutions are mixed, a chemical reaction takes place. The hydrogen ion from the hydrochloric acid combines with the hydroxide ion (OH^-) from the sodium hydroxide to form water—the (l) following the formula for water shows that it is a liquid. The sodium ions and chlorine ions combine to form sodium chloride, or common salt:

$$\text{HCl (aq)} \quad + \text{NaOH (aq)} \rightarrow \quad \text{NaCl (aq)} \quad + \text{H}_2\text{O (l)}$$

| hydrochloric | sodium | sodium chloride | water |
| acid | hydroxide | (a salt) | |

This is exactly what Arrhenius said would happen. The hydrochloric acid donates a hydrogen ion and the sodium hydroxide accepts the hydrogen ion. But where Arrhenius' definition of a base breaks down is when a substance does not have hydroxide ions to give.

Baking soda (NaHCO_3), for example, acts like a base but has no hydroxide ions. When baking soda is dissolved in water, it breaks down into a sodium ion and an ion of hydrogen carbonate (HCO_3^-):

$$\text{NaHCO}_3 \text{ (aq)} \quad \rightarrow \text{Na}^+ \text{ (aq)} + \quad \text{HCO}_3^- \text{ (aq)}$$

| sodium hydrogen | sodium | hydrogen carbonate |
| carbonate (baking soda) | ion | ion |

If baking soda is added to hydrochloric acid, however, it does accept a hydrogen ion. So, according to Brønsted and Lowry's theories, baking soda is a base:

$$\text{HCl (aq)} \quad + \text{NaHCO}_3 \text{ (aq)} \rightarrow \quad \text{NaCl} \quad + \text{H}_2\text{CO}_3$$

| hydrochloric | baking | sodium | carbonic |
| acid | soda (base) | chloride (salt) | acid |

(Scientists refer to baking soda as sodium hydrogen carbonate, also known as sodium bicarbonate.)

The Brønsted-Lowry definition of an acid is essentially the same as Arrhenius' idea: An acid is any substance that releases a hydrogen ion. Their idea has come to be known as the Brønsted-Lowry theory of acids and bases.

Lewis Acids and Bases

In 1923, the same year that Brønsted and Lowry came up with their idea of what acids and bases were, an American chemist named Gilbert Newton Lewis began to work on his own acid-base theory. Lewis defined acid as any substance that accepted an electron pair. A base, on the other hand, is any substance that donates an electron pair.

To understand Lewis' ideas of acids and bases, it is necessary to understand a little bit about **valence electrons** and the **octet rule**. Valence electrons are those electrons on the highest energy level of an atom. These electrons are the ones that are active in the chemical bonding of atoms during a chemical reaction. Take the atoms hydrogen and oxygen that make up water, for example. A hydrogen atom has an atomic number of one. Therefore, a hydrogen atom has one proton in its nucleus. (The atomic number of an element is equal to the number of protons in an atom of that element.) If a hydrogen atom has one proton, it must also have one electron so that the atom is electrically neutral. A hydrogen atom's single electron is found in the first, and only, energy level that surrounds the atom's nucleus. Because the electron is in the highest energy level, that electron is hydrogen's valence electron.

ACIDS IN ALCHEMY

The alchemists of the Middle Ages were no strangers to acids. In fact, *aqua fortis*, which literally means "strong water," is basically nitric acid. Alchemists used *aqua fortis* to dissolve certain metals. Specifically, they used it to separate silver (which would dissolve in *aqua fortis*) from gold (which would not).

Aqua regia, or "royal water," on the other hand, could dissolve gold. It turns out that the alchemist's *aqua regia* was a mixture of concentrated hydrochloric and nitric acids. Either of these acids alone will not affect gold, but a mixture of the two dissolves the precious metal.

Gilbert Newton Lewis devised what would come to be called the Lewis dot diagram. A Lewis dot diagram (or electron dot diagram) shows the symbol of an atom as the "kernel" of the atom (the nucleus plus any energy levels that contain electrons that are not on the highest energy level) and dots to represent the valence electrons. So the Lewis dot diagram of hydrogen would show the symbol for the element hydrogen and a single dot to illustrate its one valence electron as follows:

$$H\cdot$$

The element oxygen, on the other hand, has an atomic number of eight. Therefore, an oxygen atom has eight protons and eight electrons. The first energy level in an atom can contain only two electrons. The second can hold as many as eight electrons. So an oxygen atom will have two electrons on its first energy level and six on its second, and outermost, energy level. Therefore, an oxygen atom has six valence electrons, as shown below:

$$\cdot \overset{\cdot\cdot}{\underset{\cdot\cdot}{O}} \cdot$$

In chemistry, the octet rule is a rule of thumb that says that atoms are at their most stable when they contain eight electrons (hence the name octet) in their highest energy level. Atoms will gain, lose, or share electrons in order to achieve this stable state. The octet rule does not apply in every situation (which is why it is called a rule of thumb instead of a law), but it is very useful to keep in mind. In many cases, the octet rule can help explain the bonding behavior of atoms.

Hydrogen and oxygen, for example, react to form water so that both elements have a stable electron configuration (which refers to the number and arrangement of electrons). If hydrogen gave up its electron to oxygen, however, the hydrogen would not be stable because it would have no electrons. So, rather than giving its electron to oxygen, it shares its electron:

$$H\cdot + \cdot \overset{..}{O} \cdot + \cdot H \rightarrow H\!-\!\overset{..}{\underset{..}{O}}\!-\!H$$

Each long dashed line on the right-hand side of the equation shows a covalent bond that has formed between a hydrogen atom and an oxygen atom. In a covalent bond, atoms share electrons in order to conform to the octet rule. Each hydrogen atom is now sharing its one electron with the oxygen atom and the oxygen atom is sharing one of its unpaired valence electrons with each hydrogen atom. This gives each hydrogen atom two electrons in its outermost energy level. With its first (and only) energy level full, the hydrogen atoms are stable, even though they do not have eight electrons (recall that the first energy level can only hold a maximum of two electrons). In return, the oxygen atom gets to share two electrons. Along with oxygen's own six valence electrons, this sharing gives the oxygen atom eight electrons on its outermost energy level and also makes it stable. This explains why every water molecule contains two atoms of hydrogen and one atom of oxygen. It also explains how acids, which donate hydrogen ions, accept an electron pair according to Lewis' definition of acids and bases. A base, according to Lewis, is any substance that donates the electron pair that the acid accepts.

CONJUGATE ACID-BASE PAIRS

According to the Brønsted-Lowry definition of acids and bases, an acid is a proton donor. The particle that is left over after an acid donates its proton, however, can now accept a proton and, therefore, can act as a base. For example, if hydrochloric acid donates its proton to the base ammonia (NH_3), the particles formed are a chlorine ion (Cl^-) and an ammonium ion (NH_4^+):

$$HCl \quad + \quad NH_3 \quad \rightleftarrows \quad Cl^- \quad + \quad NH_4^+$$

hydrochloric   ammonia   chlorine   ammonium

acid   ion   ion

The chlorine ion can now accept a proton (and become hydrochloric acid again). If the chlorine can accept a proton, according to the Brønsted-Lowry definition, it is a base. Chemists actually call this chlorine ion the **conjugate base** of hydrochloric acid. Any time an acid gives up its proton, the substance that is left over can act as a base. So every acid has a conjugate base.

The double arrow in the chemical equation above indicates that the reaction is reversible. This means that while some hydrochloric acid molecules are breaking down into hydrogen and chlorine ions, some ions are also combining to produce hydrochloric acid. The same ongoing, continuous process also occurs to the ammonia molecules. Some ammonia molecules accept a hydrogen ion to become an ammonium ion while some ammonium ions give up a hydrogen ion to become an ammonia molecule.

It works the same way for bases. Every base has a **conjugate acid**. The ammonium in the above equation, for example, is ammonia's conjugate acid. The ammonium ion has an extra proton that it can donate, making it an acid.

Here are a few other examples of conjugate acid-base pairings:

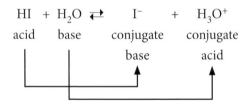

$$HI \quad + \quad H_2O \quad \rightleftarrows \quad I^- \quad + \quad H_3O^+$$

acid   base   conjugate   conjugate

                          base   acid

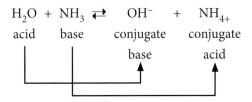

$$H_2O + NH_3 \rightleftharpoons OH^- + NH_{4+}$$

acid   base   conjugate   conjugate
                    base   acid

In the two equations above, notice that water is acting as an acid in one instance and as a base in the other. Substances like water that can act as an acid or a base depending on the circumstances are called **amphoteric** substances. The word comes from the Greek prefix *ampho-,* which means "both." Water is the most common amphoteric substance, but amino acids, proteins, and some metal oxides—such as aluminum oxide (Al_2O_3) and zinc oxide (ZnO), for example—can also act as amphoteric substances.

Determining Acids and Bases

The simplest acids are composed of just two elements. Such acids are called **binary acids**. When naming a binary acid, the prefix *hydro-* is used. The ending of the second element (the nonmetal) is changed to *-ic* and the word "acid" is added. For example, the chemical formula for hydrochloric acid is HCl. HCl is made up of two elements—hydrogen and chlorine (a nonmetal). The H stands for the element hydrogen and the Cl stands for the element chlorine. To name this acid, add the prefix *hydro-* and change the ending of chlorine to *-ic* and then add the word "acid." The result is hydrochloric acid. Another example, hydrobromic acid, which has the chemical formula HBr, gets its name because it is made up of the elements hydrogen and bromine. Hydroiodic acid (HI) is an acid containing the elements hydrogen and iodine.

Other acids are made up of more than two elements and often contain **polyatomic ions**. Polyatomic ions are collections of two or more atoms that carry a charge and are chemically bonded to one another so that they act as a single unit. The ions SO_4^{2-} and NO_3^- are examples of polyatomic ions. The ion SO_4^{2-} is called a sulfate ion. The chemical formula NO_3^- stands for a nitrate ion. To name an acid that contains a polyatomic ion which ends in -*ate*, change the -*ate* ending to -*ic* and add the word acid. Therefore, H_2SO_4 stands for sulfuric acid and HNO_3 stands for nitric acid.

Chemical formulas are a shorthand method of representing a chemical compound. By looking at a chemical formula, a scientist can tell how many atoms of each element are present in that particular compound. For example, by looking at the chemical symbols in H_2SO_4, a chemist knows that the compound is made up of three different elements—hydrogen (H), sulfur (S), and oxygen (O). A chemist can also tell how many atoms of each element are present in the compound by looking at the subscripts in the chemical formula. H_2SO_4, for example, contains two atoms of hydrogen, one atom of sulfur (the one is not written, it is just understood to be there), and four atoms of oxygen. When sulfuric acid is dissolved in water, however, it does not break down into hydrogen, sulfur, and oxygen. Instead, it breaks down into hydrogen ions and sulfate ions. The sulfate ions stay together as one unit:

$$H_2SO_4 \text{ (aq)} \rightarrow 2\,H^+ + SO_4^{2-}$$

$$\text{sulfuric acid} \qquad \text{hydrogen ion} \qquad \text{sulfate ion}$$

The numeral two written in front of the hydrogen ion shows that for every molecule of sulfuric acid, two hydrogen ions and one sulfate ion (again, the one is understood) are released. At least this is the way it works in theory. In reality, hydrogen ions do not really just float in water, but instead pretty quickly attach themselves to a water molecule. The molecule formed, H_3O^+, is called a hydronium ion:

$$\text{H}^+ \quad + \text{ H}_2\text{O} \quad \rightarrow \quad \text{H}_3\text{O}^+$$

hydrogen   water   hydronium

ion   ion

The hydronium ion is really the ion that gives an acid its proper-ties. For the sake of simplicity, however, most chemists ignore the hydronium ion in favor of just saying a hydrogen ion (or proton) and writing H^+ in a chemical equation.

Nitric acid acts in a similar manner to sulfuric acid when it is dissolved in water:

$$\text{HNO}_3\,(\text{aq}) \quad \rightarrow \quad \text{H}^+ \quad + \text{NO}_3^-$$

nitric   hydrogen   nitrate

acid   ion   ion

For every molecule of nitric acid dissolved in water, one hydrogen ion and one nitrate ion are produced.

There are also some polyatomic ions that end with the letters -ite. SO_3^{2-} and NO_2^- are examples of polyatomic ions with -ite end-ings. The ion SO_3^{2-} is called a sulfite ion and NO_2^- is a nitrite ion. To name an acid that contains a polyatomic ion that ends in -ite, change the -ite to -ous and add the word "acid." Therefore, the name for H_2SO_3 is sulfurous acid and HNO_2 is nitrous acid.

Naming bases is a little more straightforward. For a base name, chemists just use the name of the chemical compound. They do the same thing for the salts that are produced when acids and bases react with one another. The salt sodium chloride (NaCl), for example, is named for the two elements that are present in the salt—sodium and chlorine. The only rule is to change the ending for the name of the nonmetal (in this case, chlorine) to -ide, giving us the name sodium chloride.

Many bases contain the polyatomic ion hydroxide (OH^-). To name a base containing this ion, name the metal first, then list the name for the polyatomic ion. For example, the name of the base NaOH is sodium hydroxide. KOH is potassium hydroxide. It is easy to tell the two substances apart when their chemical names or formulas are given, but both sodium hydroxide and potassium hydroxide have the same common name—lye. This can be very confusing. Therefore, to distinguish the two chemicals, the common names soda lye (for NaOH) and potash lye (for KOH) are used.

Not all bases contain hydroxide, however. For example, Na_2CO_3 is a base, but its name is sodium carbonate. Baking soda, which has a chemical formula of $NaHCO_3$, is also a base. The scientific name for baking soda is sodium hydrogen carbonate (hydrogen carbonate is the name of the polyatomic ion).

NH_3 is also a common base. The elements that make up NH_3—nitrogen and hydrogen—are both nonmetals. When two nonmetals chemically bond to one another, a covalent bond is formed. To name covalent compounds, the prefixes *mono-*, *di-*, *tri-*, and so on are used to designate the number of atoms present in the compound. In the chemical compound NH_3, there is one nitrogen atom and three hydrogen atoms. The prefix *mono-* is left off if there is only one atom of the first element in the compound. So the scientific name for NH_3 is nitrogen trihydride. This compound has been known for a very long time, before anyone had any idea what its chemical formula was. With no knowledge of its chemical formula, the compound was named ammonia. Even today, nitrogen trihydride is still mostly referred to by its common name—ammonia.

Using the same logic, the chemical compound H_2O can also be named using the prefixes *mono-* and *di-*. Because there is only one oxygen atom in water and the oxygen is the second element in the compound, the prefix *mono-* is used. The scientific name for H_2O is dihydrogen monoxide. Of course, this compound is also much better known by its common name—water.

SELF-IONIZATION OF WATER

Even at room temperature, water molecules are in constant motion. Sometimes, the collision between water molecules can be so energetic that a hydrogen ion is transferred from one water molecule to another. This leads to one hydronium ion and one hydroxide ion being formed.

$$H_2O \rightleftharpoons H_3O^+ + OH^-$$

water   hydronium   hydroxide
ion   ion

This process is called the self-ionization of water. Again, the double arrow shows that this reaction is reversible. At any given time, some water molecules are being broken down into hydronium ions and hydroxide ions. At the same time, some hydronium ions and hydroxide ions are bonding together to form water molecules. When the forward reaction (water ionizing) and the backward reaction (ions bonding to form water) occur at the same rate, the system is said to be in **dynamic equilibrium**. The reaction is in equilibrium because there is a balance between the forward and backward reactions. It is dynamic because it is constantly changing.

In pure water, the numbers of hydronium ions and hydroxide ions are equal. If an acid is added to the water, the number of hydronium ions increases. If a base is added, the number of hydroxide ions goes up (and the number of hydrogen ions goes down). When the concentration of hydrogen ions and hydroxide ions in an aqueous solution are multiplied together, their product is always equal to 1.0×10^{-14} (mol/L)^2. So if the number of hydrogen ions goes up, the number of hydroxide ions must go down. Likewise, if the number of hydroxide ions is increased, the number of hydrogen ions must go down. Because an acid adds hydrogen ions to a solution, the concentration of hydrogen ions in an acid must be higher than 1.0×10^{-7} (mol/L)^2.

The unit mol/L stands for moles per liter. A mole is a measurement that chemists use to state the amount of a substance. One mole is equal to 6.02×10^{23} of anything. For example, 6.02×10^{23} atoms of carbon are equal to 1 mole (mol) of carbon. One mole of hydrogen ions would equal 6.02×10^{23} hydrogen ions. And 6.02×10^{23} sandwiches would equal 1 mole of sandwiches. Using hydrogen ion and hydroxide ion concentrations in moles per liter can be cumbersome, however. Instead, chemists use the pH of a solution to describe the hydrogen and hydroxide ion concentrations.

WHAT IS PH?

The pH scale was invented in 1909 by a Danish biochemist named Sören Sörensen (1868–1939). The pH of a substance is a measure of its acidity. Because acids donate hydrogen ions, when they are added to a solution they increase its hydrogen ion concentration. The addition of a base decreases the hydrogen ion concentration in a substance because bases accept hydrogen ions.

The pH of a solution is related to the hydrogen ion concentration by the following mathematical formula:

$$pH = -\log [H^+]$$

The abbreviation "log" stands for logarithm. In mathematics, a logarithm is the power (also called an exponent) to which a number (called the base) has to be raised to get a particular number. In other words, it is the number of times the base (this is the mathematical base, not a chemical base) must be multiplied times itself to get a particular number. For example, if the base number is 10 and 1,000 is the number trying to be reached, the logarithm is 3 because 10 x 10 x 10 equals 1,000. Another way to look at this is to put the number 1,000 into scientific notation:

$$1,000 = 1.00 \times 10^3$$

Concentration of hydrogen ions compared to distilled water	Approximate pH	Examples
10,000,000	0	battery acid
1,000,000	1	stomach acid
100,000	2	lemon juice
10,000	3	vinegar
1,000	4	soft drink
100	5	coffee
10	6	milk
0	7	distilled ("pure") water
1/10	8	egg whites
1/100	9	toothpaste
1/1,000	10	antacids
1/10,000	11	household ammonia
1/100,000	12	calcium hydroxide (slaked lime)
1/1,000,000	13	bleach
1/10,000,000	14	drain cleaner

Acids — rows pH 0 through 6
Neutral — pH 7
Bases — rows pH 8 through 14

Source: Ridmond River County Council
© Infobase Publishing

The chart above highlights common examples of acids and bases and their approximate pH, which correspond to their concentrations of hydrogen ions compared to distilled water. The number of hydrogen ions decreases as the pH increases.

The exponent (or power) to which the base number (10) has to be raised is the logarithm. To find the pH of a substance, the negative of the logarithm of the hydrogen ion concentration must be taken.

For example, if the hydrogen ion concentration of a solution is 1.00×10^{-3} moles per liter, the logarithm is -3. The pH is the negative of the logarithm, or 3. Determining the pH by looking at the exponent only works if the coefficient is 1, however. In other words, if the hydrogen ion concentration is 1.00×10^{-12} moles per liter, the pH is 12. However, if the hydrogen ion concentration is 6.88×10^{-12} moles per liter, the pH is 11. To determine the logarithm of a number when the coefficient is not 1, a table of logarithms or a calculator is needed.

The pH and the hydrogen ion concentration are inversely related. In other words, the higher the hydrogen ion concentration, the lower the pH. Therefore, the lower a solutions's pH, the more acidic it is because there are more hydrogen ions in the solution. A higher pH, on the other hand, indicates fewer hydrogen ions and more hydroxide ions. Therefore, the solution is more alkaline, or basic. A solution with an equal number of hydrogen ions and hydroxide ions is neutral. In a neutral solution, the concentrations of hydrogen and hydroxide ions are both 1.00×10^{-7} moles per liter (remember that the product must equal 1.00×10^{-14} $[mol/L]^2$). Therefore, a neutral solution has a pH of 7. A substance with a pH of 7 is neither acidic nor basic. Acids have a pH lower than 7 and bases have a pH higher than 7. The pH scale ranges from 0 to 14.

Litmus Paper

Litmus paper changes color in the presence of an acid or a base. Substances like litmus paper are called **acid-base indicators**. An acid-base indicator responds to the concentration of hydrogen ions in a solution by changing color. Litmus paper is a very common acid-base indicator. It turns blue if the pH is above 8.2. Therefore, if litmus turns blue, it means the substance is a base.

Litmus turns red below a pH of 4.5. Substances that turn litmus red are, therefore, acids.

Litmus paper is made from lichens. Lichens are a unique type of plant. Instead of being one type of organism, lichens are actually made up of two types of organisms—fungi and algae. The fungi and algae live together in a symbiotic relationship. Lichens live in

PLANT INDICATORS

Litmus is not the only plant material that turns a different color in response to acidic or basic conditions. For example, when red cabbage or beets are boiled, the solids can be separated from the liquid. The liquid is then cooled for use as an acid-base indicator. Red cabbage juice is red or purple in acidic conditions, while bases cause it to turn blue or yellow. When a solution is neutral, the juice is a bluish-purple.

Gardeners can tell if a hydrangea bush is growing in acidic or basic soil—even without a soil testing kit—by just looking at the plant's flowers. The flowers of a hydrangea bush are blue if the plant is growing in acidic soil. The flowers are pink if the soil is alkaline. It is not actually the hydrogen ion concentration, however, that makes the flowers blue, but rather aluminum (Al) compounds. In soils with a pH of 5.5 or lower, aluminum compounds are in a form that the plant can absorb. A high aluminum concentration in the flowers makes them blue. In soil where the pH is 6.5 or higher, however, the aluminum compounds are not available in the correct form and the plant cannot absorb them. Without the aluminum compounds, the flowers are pink.

If gardeners want blue flowers, they often add aluminum sulfate [$Al_2(SO_4)_3$] or sulfur to the soil to reduce the pH to 5.5. For people who prefer pink, lime (a base) is used to bring the pH to 6.5 or above. Occasionally, a hydrangea bush will produce purple flowers. This color is difficult to obtain, however. Purple flowers only come about when the pH is between many different types of environments—from the sides of trees and walls to sidewalks, and even under water. They are often used to monitor the health of the environment they live in because they are sensitive to many different types of pollution.

Litmus paper comes in two varieties—blue and red. Blue litmus paper is made by soaking the paper in a solution containing lichens

A hydrangea bush's flowers turn blue if it is being grown in acidic soil; the flowers are pink if the soil is alkaline, or basic. Purple flowers grow in soil that is in a narrow midrange between acidic and basic.

the 5.5 that produces blue flowers and the 6.5 that results in pink flowers. Therefore, to get purple flowers, a very narrow range of pH must be maintained.

and then allowing it to dry. Red litmus paper requires an additional step. Before it is dried, the paper is exposed to a tiny amount of sulfuric or hydrochloric acid. This turns the blue litmus paper red. When red litmus paper is exposed to a base, it turns back to its natural color—blue. When blue litmus paper is placed into an acid, it turns red.

Phenolphthalein

Phenolphthalein is another acid-base indicator. It is often used by magicians (and chemistry teachers) to perform a trick that turns "water" into "wine." In acidic and neutral conditions, phenolphthalein is colorless and looks like water. A pH of approximately 8.3, however, turns phenolphthalein a deep reddish-violet color. In basic conditions, phenolphthalein looks like red wine.

To perform the classic magic trick, the water is prepared ahead of time by adding a small amount of sodium hydroxide. When sodium hydroxide dissolves in water, it results in a colorless solution that still looks like plain water. The sodium hydroxide also, however, makes the solution slightly basic. Another glass, the "wine" glass, is prepared with a few drops of phenolphthalein in the bottom of the glass. When the alkaline solution is poured into the glass containing the phenolphthalein, the "water" turns a deep wine-red color. A third glass, containing a few drops of an acid (such as vinegar, for example), is used to turn the "wine" back into "water." When the alkaline "wine" is added to the acid, the phenolphthalein reverts back to its colorless state.

What makes indicators change color in the presence of acids and bases? A color change is often the sign that a chemical reaction has occurred, and this is no exception: Acid-base indicators are actually acids or bases themselves. They change colors because the acid and its conjugate base (or the base and its conjugate acid) are different colors. For example, suppose an acidic indicator, abbreviated HIn (this is not really a chemical formula, it is just a way to show an indicator that has hydrogen ions to donate), is dissolved in water. It

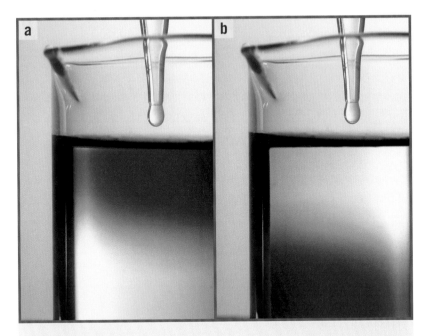

Phenolphthalein is an acid-base indicator that can be used for the trick of turning "water" into "wine." Phenolphthalein looks like water in acidic and neutral conditions, but turns to a deep reddish-violet, wine-like color when a base is added to it (a). Adding an acid, such as vinegar, to the "wine" solution turns it clear again (b).

will break down into hydrogen ions and indicator ions, abbreviated In^- (again, this is not a true chemical formula but stands for the part of the indicator molecule that was attached to the hydrogen ions):

$$HIn \rightleftharpoons H^+ + In^-$$

acid   hydrogen   conjugate
                  ion   base

Notice that this is a reversible reaction. If the acidic indicator (HIn) is phenolphthalein and an acid is introduced into the solution, more hydrogen ions are available to react with the In^- molecule. This shifts the reaction more to the left-hand side, and therefore produces more acid. When phenolphthalein is in its acidic form, it is colorless. When a base is added, hydroxide ions react with the hydrogen ions to form water. This means that there are fewer hydrogen ions to react with the In⁻ molecule. The equation is, therefore, shifted more to the right. The conjugate base of the phenolphthalein molecule is red-violet.

The reason the two forms of phenolphthalein are different colors is because the chemical reaction changes the shape of the phenolphthalein molecule. In other words, the molecule has a different shape under acidic conditions than it does under basic conditions. The different shapes absorb and reflect different wavelengths of light. Our eyes see different wavelengths of visible light as different colors.

Measuring Exact pH

Although litmus paper, cabbage juice, and phenolphthalein can indicate whether a substance is acidic or basic, they have limitations in that they cannot determine an exact pH. To do this, an acid-base indicator called universal indicator can be used. Universal indicator is actually a mixture of several different acid-base indicators (usually phenolphthalein, methyl red, bromthymol blue, and thymol blue). This mixture produces a wide range of colors to indicate different pHs. Under very acidic conditions, universal indicator is red. It turns orange and then yellow between the pHs of 3 to 6. It is green at neutral pH and turns greenish-blue as a solution becomes more alkaline. In very basic conditions, universal indicator turns a dark purple color.

A pH meter is another way to measure the exact pH of a substance. Of all the ways to measure pH, using a pH meter is the most precise. A pH meter sends an electrical current through the sample being tested. Because electricity is a flow of negatively charged electrons, the force of the electron current is directly proportional to the hydrogen ion content of the sample. In other words, the more current (or electrons) carried though the sample, the more protons

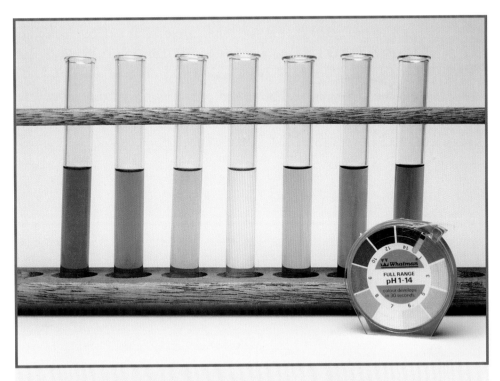

An acid-base indicator called universal indicator can show the exact pH of a substance. Adding a small amount of universal indicator to a solution changes the color of the solution. Each color represents a different pH.

(or positive hydrogen ions) that are present in the sample and the more acidic the sample.

A pH meter contains two different types of electrodes—a sensing electrode and a reference electrode. The sensing electrode is a thin glass bulb that can detect protons in the solution, which causes the voltage of the sensing electrode to change depending on the hydrogen ion concentration. The reference electrode, which is often located inside the glass bulb of the sensing electrode, is not sensitive to hydrogen ions at all. Instead, the reference electrode has a constant voltage. The pH meter calculates the difference in voltage between the sensing electrode and the reference electrode and converts this difference into a pH, which is then displayed on a screen. A pH meter is very similar to a voltmeter, but instead of showing volts as an output, it shows pH. Differences in pH are due to the way different acids and bases break down in water.

Acids and Bases in Chemistry

When placed in water, some acids and bases completely ionize, or dissociate into their ions—but others do not. Acids and bases that completely ionize are called **strong acids** and **strong bases**. Strong acids are defined as acids that have a pH of 0–4. Strong bases have pH values of 10–14. On the other hand, **weak acids** and **weak bases** do not disassociate completely in water. This leads to a pH value that is closer to neutral, because some of the hydrogen ions are still attached to other atoms, decreasing the hydrogen ion concentration.

The breakdown of any acid or base in water to form its ions is a reversible reaction. Hydrochloric acid, for example, is a strong acid that dissociates completely to form hydrogen ions and chlorine ions:

$$\text{HCl (aq)} \rightleftharpoons \text{H}^+ + \text{Cl}^-$$

hydrochloric	hydrogen	chlorine
acid	ion	ion

This reaction is much more successful to the right (hydrochloric acid molecules breaking down into ions) than it is to the left (ions combining to form hydrochloric acid molecules). Some hydrogen ions and chlorine ions, however, will reunite to form hydrochloric acid again. Hydrochloric, sulfuric, and nitric acids are the most common strong acids. Sodium, potassium, and calcium hydroxides are all strong bases. In fact, with one exception, all of the bases that contain metals from Group IA and Group IIA on the periodic table are strong bases. The exception is beryllium hydroxide (BeOH).

In a weak acid or base, the backwards reaction (where ions join to form the acid or base) occurs more often than it does in a strong acid or base. Therefore, with a weak acid or base, some hydrogen and hydroxide ions are released, but there are many more molecules of intact acid or base than there would be with a strong acid or base. Most acids and bases are weak. They do not completely break down in water.

Chemists have calculated the extent to which most acids and bases will dissociate in water. This mathematical value is called the acid dissociation constant (K_a) for acids and the base dissociation constant (K_b) for bases. The higher the value for K_a or K_b, the more the acid or base dissociates in water and the stronger it is.

Hydrochloric acid has the highest K_a on this list and is, therefore, the strongest acid listed. Lithium hydroxide is the strongest base listed. Because K_a and K_b values are often very large or very small numbers, chemists have converted them into an easier form called pK_a and pK_b.

The calculation for pK_a bears a strong resemblance to the calculation to pH. That is because the relationship between pK_a

TABLE 4.1: DISSOCIATION CONSTANTS FOR COMMON ACIDS AND BASES

K_a FOR SOME COMMON ACIDS (mol/dm³)		K_b FOR SOME COMMON BASES (mol/dm³)	
Hydrochloric acid (HCl)	1.3×10^6	Lithium hydroxide (LiOH)	2.3
Nitric acid (HNO$_3$)	2.4×10^1	Potassium hydroxide (KOH)	3.1×10^{-1}
Phosphoric acid (H$_3$PO$_4$)	7.1×10^{-3}	Sodium hydroxide (NaOH)	6.3×10^{-1}
Boric acid (H$_3$BO$_3$)	5.8×10^{-10}	Ammonia (NH$_3$)	1.8×10^{-5}

and K_a is exactly the same as the relationship between pH and the hydrogen ion concentration:

$$pK_a = -\log K_a \qquad pK_b = -\log K_b$$

Like pH, pK_a and pK_b values have no units. Also like pH, the stronger the acid, the lower the pK_a value. Likewise, the lower the pK_b value, the stronger the base.

The terms weak and strong do not have the same meaning as the terms **dilute** and **concentrated**. The strength of an acid or a base is completely dependant on how it dissociates in water. A concentrated or dilute solution, on the other hand, depends on how

TABLE 4.2: pK_a FOR COMMON ACIDS AND pK_b FOR COMMON BASES

pK_a FOR SOME COMMON ACIDS		pK_b FOR SOME COMMON BASES	
Hydrochloric acid (HCl)	−6	Lithium hydroxide (LiOH)	−0.36
Nitric acid (HNO$_3$)	−1.4	Potassium hydroxide (KOH)	0.5
Phosphoric acid (H$_3$PO$_4$)	2.1	Sodium hydroxide (NaOH)	0.2
Boric acid (H$_3$BO$_3$)	9.2	Ammonia (NH$_3$)	4.7

much acid or base is in the solution relative to the amount of water. Making a concentrated solution of a weak acid or base is possible by simply adding more acid or base to the solution. Likewise, a dilute solution of a strong acid or base can be made by adding more water to the solution. If more water is added to a solution, the solution is more dilute because there are fewer dissociated ions per unit of water. Regardless of how much water is in a solution, however, a strong acid or base will completely dissociate into its ions and a weak acid or base will not.

NEUTRALIZATION REACTIONS

When acids and bases come into contact with one another, a chemical reaction called a **neutralization reaction** takes place. A neutralization reaction is a **double displacement reaction**. In a double displacement reaction, the positive ions from one reactant take the place of the positive ions in the other reactant. For example, if hydrochloric acid and sodium hydroxide react with one another, the positive sodium ion in sodium hydroxide will take the place of the hydrogen ion in the hydrochloric acid:

$$HCl \;+\; NaOH \;\rightarrow\; NaCl \;+\; H_2O$$

| hydrochloric acid | sodium hydroxide | sodium chloride | water |

The positive and negative ions in each reactant have switched partners to produce the products—water and a salt.

Beyond Sodium Chloride

Water is always one product of a neutralization reaction. The other product is a salt. In the reaction of hydrochloric acid and sodium hydroxide, the salt is sodium chloride, which is, literally, table salt. Not all acid-base reactions make sodium chloride, but they do make a salt. Salts are **ionic compounds**. An ionic compound is a compound that is made up of cations (positively

SODA-ACID FIRE EXTINGUISHERS

A soda-acid fire extinguisher uses a chemical reaction between an acid (sulfuric acid) and a base (baking soda) to produce a jet of water that can put out a fire. The fire extinguisher has a glass vial that contains the sulfuric acid. The extinguisher's body contains a baking soda solution. When the operator pushes a plunger down to break the vial, the two chemicals react, and water and carbon dioxide gas are produced. This action activates the fire extinguisher.

$$H_2SO_4 \; + \; 2\,NaHCO_3 \; \rightarrow \; Na_2SO_4 \; + \; 2\,H_2O \; + \; 2\,CO_2\,(g)$$

| sulfuric acid | sodium bicarbonate (baking soda) | sodium sulfate (a salt) | water | carbon dioxide gas |

As the gas pressure inside the extinguisher increases, it pushes a jet of water out of the extinguisher's nozzle. Because soda acid extinguishers expel water, they should only be used on class "A" fires. Class "A" fires are those that involve wood, paper, cardboard, and cloth. Soda-acid fire extinguishers should never be used on electrical or grease fires because the water they use can cause these kinds of fires to spread and burn out of control.

In a soda-acid fire extinguisher, a chemical reaction between an acid (sulfuric acid) and a base (baking soda) produces a jet of water that can put out certain kinds of fires.

charged ions) and anions (negatively charged ions). The charges in an ionic compound balance each other out so that the compound is neutral.

When a strong acid such as sulfuric acid is dissolved in water, it completely dissociates into ions:

$$H_2SO_4 \text{ (aq)} \rightleftharpoons 2\,H^+ + SO_4{}^{2-}$$

sulfuric	hydrogen	sulfate
acid	ions	ion

The number 2 in front of the hydrogen ion means that for every molecule of sulfuric acid that dissociates, two hydrogen ions are produced.

Likewise, when a strong base such as potassium hydroxide dissolves in water, it dissociates into its ions, too:

$$KOH \text{ (aq)} \rightleftharpoons K^+ + OH^-$$

potassium	potassium	hydroxide
hydroxide	ion	ion

Potassium hydroxide produces one potassium ion and one hydroxide ion for each molecule of potassium hydroxide that dissociates.

Remember that an acid-base reaction is a double displacement reaction. Therefore, if sulfuric acid and potassium hydroxide are mixed, the positive ions trade places. The hydrogen ions from the sulfuric acid will react with the negative hydroxide ions to form water. Because a hydrogen ion has a charge of +1 and a hydroxide ion has a charge of −1, they bond in a 1:1 ratio:

$$H^+ + OH^- \rightarrow H^2O$$

hydrogen	hydroxide	water
ion	ion	

The positive potassium ions from the potassium hydroxide will react with the negative sulfate ion from the sulfuric acid. Because the sulfate ion has a charge of –2 and a potassium ion has a charge of +1, two potassium ions are required to balance out the –2 charge and to make the compound neutral:

$$2\ K^+ \quad +\ SO_4^{-2} \ \rightarrow \quad K_2SO_4$$

potassium	sulfate	potassium
ions	ion	sulfate

The subscript after potassium in the chemical formula for potassium sulfate shows that two potassium ions are needed. Potassium sulfate is a salt. When the two equations are put together (as they would occur when the acid and base are mixed together), they represent the double displacement neutralization reaction that occurs between sulfuric acid and potassium hydroxide:

$$H_2SO_4\ +\ 2\ KOH \ \rightarrow \quad K_2SO_4 \quad +\ 2\ H_2O$$

sulfuric	potassium	potassium	water
acid	hydroxide	sulfate (a salt)	

BALANCED CHEMICAL EQUATIONS

In a chemical equation, like the one for the reaction between sulfuric acid and potassium hydroxide, the **reactants** (the substances being mixed together) are always written on the left-hand side of the equation. The **products** (the substances made when the reactants react with each other) are placed on the right-hand side of the equation. Atoms cannot be made or destroyed in a chemical reaction, only rearranged. This is called the **law of conservation of matter**. Therefore, there must always be the same number of atoms of each element on the reactant side of the equation as there are on the product side.

To balance a chemical equation, the chemical formulas for the reactants are first written on the left-hand side of the equation. For example, in the reaction between hydrochloric acid and sodium hydroxide, the chemical formulas are HCl and NaOH, respectively. Remember that if an acid starts with the prefix *hydro-*, it is a binary acid. That means that hydrochloric acid is made up of only two

SWIMMING POOL pH

Swimming pools must be kept around a neutral pH in order for people to swim in them comfortably. Swimming pool water that is too acidic can burn a swimmer's eyes or nose. It also makes the skin dry and itchy and destroys bathing suits much faster than a neutral pH. Acidic water not only destroys bathing suits, it can dissolve the materials used to build the pool, such as marble or plaster.

By attacking these materials, acidic water causes the pool walls to become rough. This is called etching. Not only is etching tough on bathing suits and tender skin, but algae like to grow on rough surfaces, too, requiring more cleaning. Acidic water also corrodes (breaks down) metal parts, such as ladders or pumps. Chlorine is added to swimming pool water to disinfect it. Chlorine, however, is released into the air faster in acidic water than it is when the water is neutral. In order for the pool to be properly disinfected, more chlorine must be added to the water.

When the water is too alkaline, swimmers experience similar physical discomfort—burning eyes and nose and itchy, dry skin. The effect on the pool, however, is different. When water is alkaline, calcium dissolved in the pool water can **precipitate** (fall) out of solution. A precipitate is a solid that forms from a solution due to a chemical reaction. This solid creates unsightly scales on the sides of the pool. Like water that is too acidic, alkaline water also affects the efficiency of the chlorine. More chlorine needs to be added to alkaline water to effectively disinfect the pool. Over time, a swimming pool that is not kept at a neutral pH can become very expensive to maintain.

elements. One of the elements must be hydrogen (or it would not be an acid). The second part of the name (-*chloric*) shows that the other element is chlorine.

Hydrogen forms ions with a +1 charge when it loses its one valence electron. Chlorine has seven valence electrons (as do all of the elements in column VIIA of the periodic table). It needs to gain

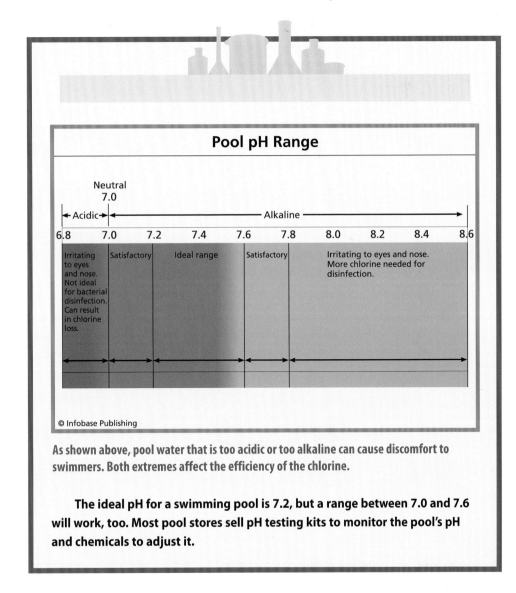

Pool pH Range

© Infobase Publishing

As shown above, pool water that is too acidic or too alkaline can cause discomfort to swimmers. Both extremes affect the efficiency of the chlorine.

The ideal pH for a swimming pool is 7.2, but a range between 7.0 and 7.6 will work, too. Most pool stores sell pH testing kits to monitor the pool's pH and chemicals to adjust it.

one electron in order to have eight valence electrons, a stable state according to the octet rule. Chlorine forms ions with a –1 charge. When the positive and negative ions come together to form the chemical compound hydrochloric acid, one hydrogen ion (with a +1 charge) and one chlorine ion (with a –1 charge) will combine to produce the electrically neutral chemical compound HCl.

Reactions involving sodium hydroxide are similar. Take a look at the periodic table. Sodium is a metal in the first column, or Group 1A, of the periodic table. Hydrogen is in Group 1A, too. Elements in the same group on the periodic table have the same number of valence electrons. Elements in Group 1A have one valence electron. Elements in Group 2A have two valence electrons, and so on. The elements on the left-hand side of the periodic table are metals. Metals form positive ions. Therefore, hydrogen ions have a charge of +1, and so do sodium ions.

Nonmetals are on the right-hand side of the periodic table. The number of the group that the nonmetal is in still represents the number of valence electrons (at least on periodic tables that retain the older group numbering system of Roman numerals). Chlorine, for example, is in Group VIIA of the periodic table, so it has seven valence electrons. In order to get eight electrons in its outer energy level, it is easier for chlorine (and other nonmetals) to gain one electron than it is to lose its seven valence electrons. Therefore, nonmetals form negative ions when they gain one or more electrons. To determine a nonmetal ion's charge from its position on the periodic table, subtract the number of valence electrons (the nonmetal's group number) from the number eight.

Note, however, that hydroxide is not on the periodic chart. That is because hydroxide is a polyatomic ion. Remember that polyatomic ions always travel together as a unit. The only way to know the charge of a polyatomic ion is to memorize it. Hydroxide has a charge of –1. So, when sodium (with a charge of +1) and a hydroxide come into contact with one another, a sodium atom gives its one valence electron to a hydroxide ion, which needs one

PERIODIC TABLE OF THE ELEMENTS

1 IA																	18 VIIIA

Atomic number → 3

Li ← Symbol

6.941 ← Atomic weight

Metals
Non-metals
Metalloids
Unknown

Numbers in parentheses are atomic mass numbers of most stable isotopes.

☆ Lanthanoids

★ Actinoids

© Infobase Publishing

Above is the periodic table of elements. Elements in the same group have the same number of valence electrons.

electron to make it stable. This electron "swapping" results in the sodium ion having a positive charge and the hydroxide ion having a negative charge. Much like the opposite poles of a magnet, the two oppositely charged ions attract each other, forming an ionic bond. The compound formed by the bonded ions is the chemical compound sodium hydroxide (NaOH). Like sodium, potassium is in Group 1A on the periodic table and it forms ions with a +1 charge. Ionic bonds between potassium ions and hydroxide ions result in the chemical compound potassium hydroxide (KOH).

Sulfuric acid, on the other hand, is made up of the polyatomic sulfate ion, which has a charge of –2. Because it has a charge of –2, a sulfate ion requires two hydrogen ions (each of which have a charge of +1) to make it stable. Therefore, sulfuric acid is made up of two hydrogen ions and one sulfate ion, and its chemical formula is H_2SO_4. The subscript number two after the symbol for hydrogen shows that there are two hydrogen atoms in the compound. The sulfate ion is made up of two elements, sulfur and oxygen. Because the sulfate ion is a polyatomic ion, however, the sulfur and four oxygen atoms react as if they are one unit.

To build the balanced chemical equation that shows the chemical reaction between sulfuric acid and potassium hydroxide, start off by writing the reactants on the left-hand side of the equation:

$$H_2SO_4 + KOH \rightarrow$$

sulfuric   potassium

acid   hydroxide

Because this is a reaction between an acid and a base, it will be a double displacement reaction, and the positive ions will switch places. The potassium ion will react with the sulfate ion, forming the salt potassium sulfate (K_2SO_4). And the hydrogen ion in the acid will react with the hydroxide ion in the base to form HOH, or water (H_2O).

$$H_2SO_4 + KOH \rightarrow K_2SO_4 + H_2O$$

sulfuric   potassium   potassium   water

acid   hydroxide   sulfate

The two hydrogen ions in sulfuric acid do not move as a group. They are not a polyatomic ion. The reason water has the formula H_2O is because oxygen is in Group VIA of the periodic table. Therefore, oxygen has six valence electrons and needs two more electrons to have eight. So, oxygen has a charge of –2. That means that two hydrogen atoms are needed to balance out oxygen's –2 charge.

However, the equation built so far does not follow the law of conservation of matter. If the number of atoms on the left-hand side and the number of atoms on the right-hand side of the equation are added up, they do not balance. Take the hydrogen atoms, for example. On the left-hand side of the equation, there are three hydrogen atoms (two in sulfuric acid and one in potassium hydroxide), but the right-hand side of the equation only has two hydrogen atoms (both of them in water):

$$H_2SO_4 \qquad + \text{ KOH } \rightarrow \text{ K}_2SO_4 \qquad + H_2O$$

3 hydrogen atoms	2 hydrogen atoms
1 sulfur atom	1 sulfur atom
5 oxygen atoms	5 oxygen atoms
1 potassium atom	2 potassium atoms

The extra hydrogen atom on the reactant side of the equation cannot just disappear. Likewise, there cannot be more potassium atoms on the right side of the equation than on the left side. Therefore, sulfuric acid and potassium hydroxide must not react in a 1:1 ratio. Instead, for every molecule of sulfuric acid that reacts, there must be two molecules of potassium hydroxide:

$$H_2SO_4 + 2 \text{ KOH } \rightarrow \text{ K}_2SO_4 + H_2O$$

A number placed in front of a compound in a chemical equation shows the number of molecules of that substance needed for a balanced chemical equation. Now, if the number of atoms of each element on the reactant side is the same as the number of those same elements on the product side of the equation, the equation is balanced:

$$H_2SO_4 \qquad + 2 \text{ KOH } \rightarrow \text{ K}_2SO_4 \qquad + H_2O$$

4 hydrogen atoms	2 hydrogen atoms
1 sulfur atom	1 sulfur atom
6 oxygen atoms	5 oxygen atoms
2 potassium atoms	2 potassium atoms

The hydrogen and oxygen atoms, however, are still out of balance. Because hydrogen and oxygen are the atoms out of balance and water contains both of those elements, try adding a 2 in front of the water on the product side of the equation:

$$H_2SO_4 \quad + 2\ KOH \rightarrow K_2SO_4 \quad\quad + 2\ H_2O$$

4 hydrogen atoms	4 hydrogen atoms
1 sulfur atom	1 sulfur atom
6 oxygen atoms	6 oxygen atoms
2 potassium atoms	2 potassium atoms

Now there are four hydrogen atoms on the reactant side (two in sulfuric acid and one in each of the two molecules of potassium hydroxide) and four hydrogen atoms on the product side (two in each of the two molecules of water). All of the other atoms have equal numbers on each side as well. Now the equation conforms to the law of conservation of matter, and it is a balanced chemical equation.

Acids and Bases in Industry

Chemists use whatever tools they can find in their laboratories to take full advantage of the properties of acids and bases. One tool they use is Kipp's apparatus, a piece of laboratory equipment that relies on acid-base chemistry to do its job. Named for its inventor, Dutch pharmacist Petrus Johannes Kipp (1808–1864), Kipp's apparatus (or gas generator) is especially useful for creating gases, such as carbon dioxide, hydrogen, or hydrogen sulfide, that the chemists can then use in other chemical reactions.

A Kipp's gas generator is made of three connected glass bowls sitting one on top of the other. The top glass bowl is removable and has a long tube that reaches through the middle bowl and into the bottom one. To produce hydrogen gas, for example, the top bowl is removed and a solid—in this case, zinc metal—is placed into the center bowl. The top bowl is then replaced. Hydrochloric acid is poured into the top bowl. The acid pours down the long tube into

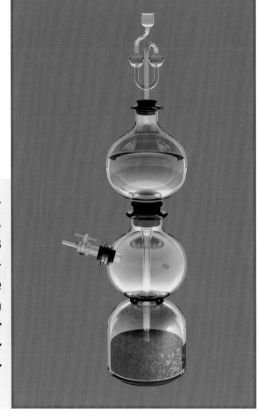

Made with three connected glass bowls, Kipp's apparatus relies on acid-base chemistry in order to produce gasses—like carbon dioxide, hydrogen, or hydrogen sulfide—for chemists to use in other chemical reactions.

the bottom bowl. When the bottom bowl is full, the acid begins to fill the middle chamber. Eventually, the acid covers the solid zinc in the center bowl, and hydrogen gas is produced in the reaction between the zinc and the hydrochloric acid:

$$2\ HCl\quad +\ Zn\ (s)\ \rightarrow\quad ZnCl_2\quad +\quad H_2\ (g)$$

hydrochloric   zinc   zinc   hydrogen gas
acid   chloride

Recall that (s) indicates a solid and (g) indicates a gas. Once gas production begins, a stoppered valve in the center bowl allows the chemist to control how much gas escapes. When the valve is opened, the gas can be collected. When it is closed, gas pressure builds up in the apparatus. As the gas pressure builds up, it forces the acid out of the center bowl and back into the bottom and top bowls. With the acid no longer in contact with the solid, gas production stops. If more gas is needed, the valve is reopened and the built-up gas is released (and collected). The acid, which is no longer held back by gas pressure, can then move from the top and bottom bowls back into the center bowl. When the acid moves back into the center bowl, it covers the solid again and produces more gas. The valve in the middle bowl can be opened and closed over and over again as gas is needed for additional chemical experiments.

To make hydrogen sulfide gas, pieces of iron(II) sulfide (instead of zinc) are placed in the center bowl of a Kipp's apparatus:

$$FeS \quad + \quad 2\,HCl \quad \rightarrow \quad FeCl_2 \quad + \quad H_2S\ (g)$$

iron(II)	hydrochloric	iron(II)	hydrogen
sulfide	acid	chloride	sulfide gas

Some metals, such as iron, can form more than one type of ion. Iron ions can either have a +2 or a +3 charge. Chemists use Roman numerals to distinguish between the two different types of iron ions. The Roman numeral II in the name of the chemical compound iron(II) sulfide means that the iron ion in this compound has a +2 charge.

Hydrogen sulfide gas is used in analytical chemistry laboratories to detect certain metal ions in a solution. If the solution contains a Group IIA metal, such as calcium, a precipitate will form when an acidic solution containing hydrogen sulfide is added to it. The precipitate forms because one of the products of the chemical reaction is insoluble (which means it does not dissolve).

Group IIIA metals, however, like aluminum, will not precipitate in an acidic hydrogen sulfide solution. They will precipitate, however, if a basic hydrogen sulfide solution is introduced. Group IA metals, on the other hand, are always soluble in a hydrogen sulfide solution, regardless of whether the solution is acidic or basic. Chemists can use these differences in solubility to identify the presence of specific metal ions.

Hydrogen sulfide is a colorless gas that smells like rotten eggs. Because of its smell, it is often called stink gas or sewer gas. It is also poisonous. Because of its toxic nature, and smell, a Kipp's apparatus generating hydrogen sulfide gas should always be kept under a fume hood.

Carbon dioxide gas can be useful in a variety of chemical experiments, too. The procedure for making carbon dioxide gas is essentially the same as it is for making hydrogen and hydrogen sulfide gases, except marble chips are used. Marble is a metamorphic rock that is created when limestone is placed under great pressure at high temperatures. Both limestone and marble are made up of calcium carbonate:

$$CaCO_3 \;+\; 2\,HCl \;\longrightarrow\; CaCl_2 \;+\; H_2O \;+\; CO_2\,(g)$$

| calcium carbonate | hydrochloric acid | calcium chloride | water | carbon dioxide gas |

ACIDS IN INDUSTRY

Chemists are not the only ones who make use of acid-base chemistry. In fact, most of the chemical manufacturing that goes on in the world is related to the production of four simple, but very useful, products—sulfuric acid, phosphoric acid, sodium hydroxide, and sodium chloride.

Sulfuric Acid

Sulfuric acid (H_2SO_4) wins the prize for being the number one chemical produced worldwide. This acid is a colorless, odorless, thick liquid. The concentrated form of the acid is also called *oleum*, the Latin word for "oil." In fact, it is so thick that it was once called "oil of vitriol, " a nickname given to the concentrated chemical because of its corrosiveness.

Indeed, as the nickname suggests, sulfuric acid is extremely corrosive in concentrated form. It can quickly eat through plastic, wood, clothing, skin, and most metals. It does not harm glass, however, so glass is used to store it. Sulfuric acid is diluted by adding it to water. Caution must be used, however, because concentrated sulfuric acid reacts violently with water to create an extremely exothermic reaction. (Remember, an exothermic reaction gives off heat.) In fact, if water is added to sulfuric acid instead of the other way around, the mixture may boil out of its flask, spilling the concentrated acid. This is why concentrated sulfuric acid (and any other acid) should always be added slowly to water and never the opposite.

Most of the sulfuric acid produced by the chemical industry is used to make fertilizers. Fertilizers are produced using phosphorous, an essential nutrient that plants need to grow well. Phosphate is found in rocks, and these rocks are more **soluble**, or more easily dissolved, in water when broken down with sulfuric acid. Treating phosphate rocks this way releases phosphorous in a form that plant roots can absorb.

People around the world rely on sulfuric acid to get them to work, school, and the grocery store as well. That is because sulfuric acid is the electrolyte used in most automobile batteries. In general, batteries work like this: Batteries are electrochemical devices that rely on a chemical reaction to produce electrons. All batteries have two terminals—a positive terminal and a negative terminal. (A battery's terminals can also be called electrodes.) Electrons build up at the battery's negative terminal (which is what makes it negative). When a wire is connected from the negative terminal of the battery through a device that requires electricity (such as a light bulb) to the positive terminal, the electrons flow through the wire to produce electricity.

An automobile battery is a type called a lead-acid storage battery. Lead-acid storage batteries rely on the chemical reaction between lead, lead dioxide, and sulfuric acid to operate. In a

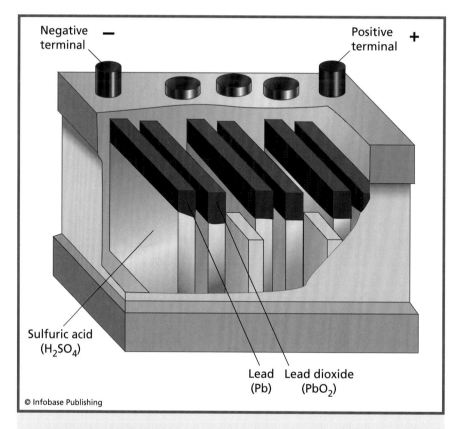

Negative terminal −

Positive terminal +

Sulfuric acid
(H_2SO_4)

Lead
(Pb) Lead dioxide
(PbO$_2$)

© Infobase Publishing

The diagram above shows a lead-acid battery, such as the kinds used in cars. This kind of battery relies on the chemical reaction between lead, lead dioxide, and sulfuric acid to operate.

lead-acid battery, the negative electrode is a plate made out of the metal lead (Pb). The positive electrode is made of the chemical compound lead dioxide (PbO_2). The electrolyte is a solution of sulfuric acid dissolved in distilled water. Remember that sulfuric acid is a strong acid. Therefore, it completely breaks down into its ions when dissolved in water.

$$H_2SO_4 \text{ (aq)} \rightleftharpoons 2\,H^+ + SO_4^{-2}$$

$$\text{sulfuric acid} \qquad \text{hydrogen ions} \qquad \text{sulfate ion}$$

The lead and lead dioxide electrodes sit in the sulfuric acid solution. The solution connects the electrodes chemically. At the negative electrode, lead reacts with sulfate ions to produce lead sulfate and an electron:

$$Pb + SO_4^{-2} \rightleftarrows PbSO_4 + e^-$$

lead   sulfate   lead   electron

ion   sulfate

At the positive terminal, lead dioxide reacts with the electrons from the lead plate and the hydrogen and sulfate ions to form lead sulfate and water:

$$PbO_2 + 4\,H^+ + SO_4^{-2} + e^- \rightleftarrows PbSO_4 + 2\,H_2O$$

lead   hydrogen   sulfate   electrons   lead   water

dioxide   ions   ion   sulfate

As a lead-acid battery discharges, lead sulfate builds up at both terminals, and water builds up in the electrolyte. The reactions in a lead-acid battery, however, are reversible. When electrical power is applied to the battery, the flow of electrons is reversed. They now flow from the positive terminal to the negative terminal.

A lead-acid storage battery is only one type of battery, however. Different batteries use different metals and electrolytes to make them work. For example, alkaline batteries (the ones found in flashlights, toys, and portable electronic devices) contain powdered zinc and manganese dioxide as their electrodes. They use an electrolyte made of an alkaline solution of potassium hydroxide. Most alkaline batteries have a finite amount of chemicals in them. Once the chemicals react with one another, they are used up, and the battery goes "dead" (is discharged) and cannot be recharged.

Sulfuric acid is often made as a byproduct of the mining of naturally occurring metal sulfide ores (mineral deposits). To purify a metal from an ore, the ore is heated in a process called smelting.

Smelting releases sulfur dioxide gas from a metal sulfide ore. Before the twentieth century, most of the sulfur dioxide expelled in the smelting process poured out of the factory's smokestacks directly into the atmosphere. Sulfur dioxide in the atmosphere, however, is a powerful greenhouse gas. Today, most of the hot sulfur dioxide gas released in the smelting process is captured, cooled, cleaned, and converted into sulfur trioxide:

$$2\ SO_2\ (g)\ +\ O_2\ (g)\ \xrightarrow{\text{catalyst}}\ 2\ SO_3\ (g)$$
$$\text{sulfur dioxide}\quad \text{oxygen}\qquad\qquad \text{sulfur trioxide}$$

This is the same reaction that occurs in Venus' atmosphere. Here on Earth, however, this reaction can be slow. To speed it up, the reaction is catalyzed. Remember, a catalyst is a chemical that speeds up a chemical reaction without taking part in the reaction itself. When chemicals are mixed together, they will only react with one another if their particles (atoms and molecules) collide. If the reactants never come into contact, a chemical reaction will not take place.

This is not the only criteria for the occurrence of a chemical reaction, however. The particles must also collide with the proper amount of energy. If they do not collide with enough energy, no chemical reaction will take place. A catalyst can facilitate a chemical reaction in two ways—it can make sure the molecules come into contact or it can lower the amount of energy needed to make a chemical reaction take place.

Platinum is usually used as the catalyst for converting sulfur dioxide into sulfur trioxide. The platinum speeds up the reaction by making it easier for molecules of sulfur dioxide and oxygen to collide. Sulfur dioxide molecules and oxygen molecules get adsorbed (or stuck to) the surface of the platinum. Because they are held so closely together, the sulfur dioxide and oxygen come into contact with each other more often and react. On the other hand, sulfur trioxide, the product of the reaction, will not stick to the platinum. It falls off while more sulfur dioxide and oxygen stick and react. The platinum is not changed or used up in any way during this reaction.

The sulfur trioxide is then bubbled though water to obtain sulfuric acid:

$$SO_3 \text{ (g)} \quad + \text{ H}_2O \text{ (l)} \rightarrow \text{ H}_2SO_4 \text{ (l)}$$

sulfur trioxide   water   sulfuric acid

 The United States produces about 40 million tons of sulfuric acid every year. That is almost 300 pounds of sulfuric acid for every American.

Phosphoric Acid

With only 10 million tons produced every year, phosphoric acid lags behind sulfuric acid in terms of production. Nevertheless, phosphoric acid is a very important chemical. Like sulfuric acid, most of the phosphoric acid made in the United States is used to manufacture agricultural fertilizers.

Phosphoric acid is produced in the reaction between sulfuric acid and calcium phosphate rock:

$$3 \text{ H}_2SO_4 \text{ (l)} + \text{ Ca}_3(PO_4)_2 \text{ (s)} \rightarrow 2 \text{ H}_3PO_4 \text{ (s)} + 3 \text{ CaSO}_4 \text{ (s)}$$

sulfuric   calcium   phosphoric   calcium

acid   phosphate   acid   sulfate

In the United States, major deposits of phosphate rock are found in Florida, North Carolina, and Idaho.

In addition to producing fertilizers, phosphoric acid is used to add the familiar tart flavor to carbonated sodas, beer, some jellies and jams, and some types of cheese. Because it dissolves iron

As seen on the side of the tub and drain stopper (*right*), a white residue known as soap scum forms when soap reacts with calcium salts present in hard water.

oxide (rust) easily, phosphoric acid is often used as a rust remover, too. Detergent manufacturers also add phosphoric acid to detergents to act as a water softener. Water softeners are chemicals that remove calcium and magnesium ions from hard water (the ions are what make the water "hard"). Without softeners, these ions precipitate out of solution when they encounter soap or detergent. This creates "soap scum" and other undesirable deposits called "scales" inside the washing machine or around the top of the bathtub. Because of its ability to dissolve these ions, phosphoric acid is often the active ingredient in cleansers that promise to

remove hard water deposits and soap scum from bathroom fix-
tures as well.

Nitric Acid

Sulfuric acid is used in the manufacture of nitric acid, too. Combining sulfuric acid with sodium nitrate produces sodium sulfate
and nitric acid:

$$2\,NaNO_3 \; + \; H_2SO_4 \; \rightarrow \; 2\,HNO_3 \; + \; Na_2SO_4$$

sodium	sulfuric	nitric	sodium
nitrate	acid	acid	sulfate

Just like sulfuric and phosphoric acids, a majority of the nitric acid
produced worldwide is used to make fertilizers. Nitric acid, however, is also used to make flares, rocket propellants, and explosives
such as nitroglycerin.

Hydrochloric Acid

Hydrochloric acid (also called muriatic acid) is often used to clean
stone buildings and swimming pools. It is also used to adjust the
pH in swimming pools and to clean steel to prepare the metal
for the hot-galvanization process. Many of the structures and
machines that people rely on every day—such as bridges, cars,
buildings, and trucks—are made of iron or steel, which also contains iron. When iron and steel are exposed to oxygen and moisture in the air, however, the iron reacts with the oxygen to form
iron oxide, or rust. Rusting is a corrosive process: If not stopped,
it can weaken the metal. The only way to stop rust is to stop the
chemical reaction. One way to do this is with galvanization, a
process designed to protect objects made of iron and steel from
the elements.

Galvanizing steel or iron parts involves dipping them into molten zinc. The zinc coats the steel or iron object, providing a barrier

The hot dip galvanization process involves dipping steal or iron parts into molten zinc. The zinc coats the parts, providing a barrier to oxygen and moisture. Exposure to oxygen and moisture can cause iron and steel to rust, which can weaken the metal. In this photo, a steel worker in Indiana performs the process.

to oxygen and moisture. Before something can be galvanized, however, it must be properly cleaned. This is where the hydrochloric acid comes into the picture. This acid is used to degrease the object and remove any rust that is already present. This process is called acid cleaning or steel-pickling. If the object is not cleaned properly, the zinc will not stick to it and the galvanizing will fail to protect the object.

Hydrochloric acid is made by dissolving hydrogen chloride gas in water. Hydrogen chloride is a colorless, poisonous gas at room temperature but it can be an extremely useful compound when dissolved in water to make hydrochloric acid.

BASES IN INDUSTRY

Historically, the alkali industry is based on limestone, or chalk. The chemical name for limestone is calcium carbonate ($CaCO_3$). It is a very common mineral in seashells. Therefore, limestone is a naturally occurring sedimentary rock formed when seas or lakes evaporate. When limestone is heated, it produces carbon dioxide

TO CATCH A CROOK

Even the police make use of acids and bases to catch criminals. For example, forensic scientists can compare soil pH found at a crime scene with trace amounts of soil found on a tire tread or shoe bottom. They also use a mixture of hydrogen peroxide and phenolphthalein called Kastle-Meyer solution to test for blood. Kastle-Meyer solution is used at a crime scene when crime scene specialists find spots they suspect could be dried blood. The solution turns bright pink in the presence of blood. If the spots turn out to be something else, such as dried tomato sauce or reddish-brown paint, the Kastle-Meyer solution remains colorless.

Criminals have even tried to use acid-base chemistry to elude capture. The 1930s bank robber John Dillinger, for example, once forced a plastic surgeon to treat his fingertips with a concentrated acid. Apparently, Dillinger thought that this would erase his fingerprints. He could have saved himself the agony, however. The acid removed only the top layer or two of his skin. The skin, along with his fingerprints, grew back. After his final shootout with the FBI, his body was identified by his fingerprints.

and calcium oxide (CaO). The common name for calcium oxide is lime:

$$CaCO_3 (s) \xrightarrow{\text{heat}} CaO (s) + CO_2 (g)$$

calcium	calcium	carbon
carbonate	oxide	dioxide
(limestone)	(lime)	gas

In the Limelight

Lime was once used in the theater. In fact, the expression "in the limelight" comes from the theater's first spotlights. Before electricity, stage lighting was produced by heating calcium oxide. Calcium oxide has a very high melting point—4,662°F (2,572°C)—so it can be heated hot enough to glow red-hot without melting. To produce a spotlight, a lens was placed in front of the glowing lime to focus the light.

Because of the high temperatures needed to make lime glow, however, producing limelight required some fancy chemistry. To get a flame hot enough, both hydrogen gas and oxygen gas (both highly flammable and potentially explosive) were needed. To make the hydrogen gas, pieces of zinc were dropped into sulfuric acid:

$$Zn (s) + H_2SO_4 (aq) \rightarrow ZnSO_4 (aq) + H_2 (g)$$

zinc	sulfuric	zinc	hydrogen
	acid	sulfate	gas

To make oxygen, potassium chlorate was heated with manganese dioxide. The manganese dioxide catalyzed the reaction and the potassium chlorate decomposed (broke down into its parts):

$$2\ KClO_3 (s) \xrightarrow{\text{MnO}_2} 2\ KCl (s) + 3\ O_2 (g)$$

potassium	potassium	oxygen
chlorate	chloride	gas

Because of the potentially explosive gases, the theater was a dangerous place to be in those days. Fire was a constant threat.

Of course, lime is no longer used to light up the stage, but it is still used today in an application that has been around for millennia—making concrete. In fact, the Great Wall of China is made of lime cement.

There is one disadvantage to having lime around, however. It must be kept completely dry wherever it is stored. The reaction between calcium oxide and water forms calcium hydroxide (or "slaked lime").

$$CaO \ + \ H_2O \ \rightarrow \ Ca(OH)_2$$

calcium	water	calcium
oxide		hydroxide
(lime)		(slaked lime)

This reaction is extremely exothermic. It can produce temperatures as high as 1,292°F (700°C). Talk about a fire hazard! In fact, in the old days, many wooden ships went up in flames when seawater leaked into the hold where the lime was kept.

Sodium Hydroxide

Sodium hydroxide (NaOH), also called lye, soda lye, or caustic soda to distinguish it from potassium hydroxide (potash lye), is another important base. Historically, lye was obtained from the ashes of wood and used to make soap. Lye, however, is an extremely caustic chemical. It can cause serious chemical burns if it comes into contact with the skin and permanent blindness if it gets into the eyes. People had to be very careful while making the soap. They also had to make sure they got the mixture of lye and animal fat (lard) correct to keep from hurting themselves and their families. Because of its caustic (corrosive) nature, sodium hydroxide is also used as the active ingredient in oven and drain cleaners.

Sodium hydroxide is made by passing an electric current through an aqueous solution of sodium chloride:

$$\overset{\text{electricity}}{2\ H_2O\ +\ 2\ NaCl\ (aq)\ \longrightarrow\ 2\ NaOH\ (aq)\ +\ Cl_2\ (g)\ +\ H_2\ (g)}$$

water   sodium   sodium   chlorine   hydrogen
          chloride   hydroxide   gas   gas

The letter "g" written after the chemical formulas for chlorine (Cl) and hydrogen show that chlorine gas and hydrogen gas are produced by the reaction.

Ammonia

Ammonia, another well known cleaner, is also used to manufacture fertilizers, nitric acid, sodium carbonate (washing soda), explosives, nylon, and baking soda. Ammonia is produced by combining nitrogen gas (obtained from the air) and hydrogen gas (obtained from natural gas) in a process called the Haber-Bosch process:

$$N_2\ (g)\ +\ 3\ H_2\ (g)\ \longrightarrow\ 2\ NH_3\ (g)$$

nitrogen   hydrogen   ammonia
                        (nitrogen trihydride)

Invented in 1909 by Fritz Haber (1868–1934), the Haber-Bosch process requires very high pressure (250 atmospheres) and a temperature of approximately 932°F (500°C). The reaction also requires a porous iron catalyst.

Scientists during Haber's time knew that three elements were absolutely necessary for optimal plant growth—potassium, phosphorous, and nitrogen. There were abundant sources of potash (potassium hydroxide) and phosphate rocks. These sources were enough to supply farmers with the potassium and phosphorous they needed to grow their crops. There was only one known source of nitrogen, however—Chilean saltpeter (sodium nitrate). Scientists also knew that 78% of the Earth's atmosphere was nitrogen gas. Therefore, Haber and other scientists set out to discover a way to turn the nitrogen in the air into soluble nitrogen compounds that plants could use.

In the beginning, Haber was successful in making a small amount of ammonia by combining nitrogen and hydrogen at normal atmospheric pressure and at a temperature of approximately 1,832°F (1,000°C) in the presence of iron filings. With the help of Carl Bosch (1874–1940), Haber soon found that temperatures above 500°C were not necessary, but high pressures were. The higher pressures sped up the reaction.

Bosch also helped develop Haber's process into an industrial process. In 1913, Haber and Bosch opened an ammonia manufacturing plant in Germany. A year later, World War I started. Saltpeter had another use besides making fertilizer. It was also necessary to make nitric acid that was used to make explosives. When the war started, the British Navy quickly cut off Germany's supply of Chilean saltpeter. If not for the Haber process, some historians estimate that Germany would have run out of nitrates to make explosives by 1916. The war lasted another two years, however, because Germany did not need to rely on outside sources of nitrates for fertilizers or explosives.

In 1918, Haber won the Nobel Prize in Chemistry for his method of making ammonia from its elements. Bosch won the same prize in 1931 for his development of high-pressure chemistry techniques. Ammonia is still the main source of nitrogen in fertilizers today.

Baking Soda
Found in everything from denture cleaners and antacids to toothpaste and bread, everyday life would be very different without

baking soda. There are several ways to make baking soda. One way is to saturate table salt with ammonia and add carbon dioxide. Baking soda, or sodium hydrogen carbonate, precipitates out of the solution:

$$NaCl\ (aq) + H_2O\ (l) + NH_3\ (g) + CO_2\ (g) \rightarrow NH_4Cl\ (aq) + NaHCO_3\ (s)$$

| sodium chloride | water | ammonia | carbon dioxide | ammonium chloride | sodium hydrogen carbonate (baking soda) |

The sodium hydrogen carbonate made in this reaction is not only good for making cookies—it can also be heated to produce sodium carbonate, or soda ash:

$$NaHCO_3 \xrightarrow{heat} Na_2CO_3 + CO_2 + H_2O$$

| sodium hydrogen carbonate | sodium carbonate (soda ash) | carbon dioxide | water |

This method of making soda ash is called the Solvay process. Discovered in 1861 by Belgian businessman Ernest Solvay (1838–1922), the Solvay process was used in the commercial production of soda ash in the 1870s, and it is still in use today. Soda ash is used in the manufacture of glass and soap. It is also used in the bleaching process for paper and cloth.

The ammonium chloride generated in this process can also be recycled by adding lime to it. The reaction between ammonium chloride and lime produces ammonia:

$$2\ NH_4Cl + CaO \rightarrow CaCl_2 + H_2O + 2\ NH_3$$

| ammonium chloride | calcium oxide (lime) | calcium chloride | water | ammonia |

MUMMY MAKING

The ancient Egyptians had another use for baking soda and soda ash. They used a naturally occurring carbonate mineral called natron to help preserve their dead for the afterlife. Natron is mainly composed of sodium carbonate (soda ash) and sodium hydrogen carbonate (baking soda). Today, we use baking soda for many of the things ancient Egyptians used natron for, including cleaning our teeth, bodies, and homes—not for preserving the dead, though.

Baking soda can also be made by combining soda ash with water and carbon dioxide:

$$Na_2CO_3 + H_2O + CO_2 \rightarrow NaHCO_3$$

| sodium carbonate (soda ash) | water | carbon dioxide | sodium hydrogen carbonate (baking soda) |

Indeed, acids and bases are very useful chemicals, and life would not be the same without them. However, strong acids and bases can also be very dangerous chemicals. Caustic, or corrosive, chemicals like strong acids and bases can burn flesh on contact. Chemical burns can be just as bad as (or even worse than) burns made by fire. Strong acids and bases disintegrate flesh by dehydrating it and then breaking down the chemical bonds that hold flesh together. The eyes and the lungs are particularly vulnerable to chemical burns.

Acids and Bases in the Human Body

Acids and bases can be dangerous chemicals outside of the body, but there are plenty of acids and bases inside the human body as well. Not only are these acids and bases not harmful to the body, but also they are absolutely necessary for it to function properly.

DIGESTION

One bodily function that relies on acids and bases is the process of digestion. During digestion, food is broken down into small molecules that the body can use. Digestion begins in the mouth when food comes into contact with an **enzyme** called amylase found in the saliva. Enzymes are the body's catalysts. They speed up chemical reactions that would otherwise be too slow to be useful to the body. Amylase breaks down starch molecules and converts them into sugars.

After the food is swallowed, the digestive process continues in the stomach where the food is attacked by stomach acid. In fact, stomach acid is concentrated hydrochloric acid. The hydrochloric acid, along with an enzyme called pepsin, breaks down proteins in the food. Pepsin can only function in the low pH environment of the stomach. The hydrochloric acid is needed to maintain the low pH that pepsin needs to function.

If acids are so corrosive, especially concentrated acids, what prevents the hydrochloric acid from eating through the stomach lining? The answer is the mucus that lines the stomach. If stomach acid seeps back into the esophagus, which does not have a mucus coating to protect it, a person can suffer from the common ailment known as heartburn. Despite its name, heartburn has nothing to do with the heart. (Certain symptoms of heart attacks, however, are unfortunately mistaken for heartburn.) Stomach acid is usually trapped in the stomach by a one-way valve called the lower esophageal sphincter (LES). The LES opens to allow food into the stomach. It also opens to allow gas out (also known as a burp). If the LES does not close properly, however, stomach acid can seep up into the esophagus. This backward flow of acid is called reflux. Because the acid is caustic, it causes the burning sensation in the esophagus. (Heartburn is also known as acid reflux.)

To prevent damage to the small intestines, stomach acid must be neutralized before food can move further down the digestive tract. A hormone called secretin in the top part of the small intestine (a section called the duodenum) monitors the pH in the small intestine. Secretin sends chemical signals to other parts of the body telling them when to release different chemicals in order to maintain the correct pH balance. For example, if secretin senses that the contents of the duodenum are too acidic, it sends a signal to the pancreas to secrete alkaline digestive juices. The alkaline digestive juices contain sodium bicarbonate. The bicarbonate neutralizes the stomach acid and keeps it from harming the small intestines.

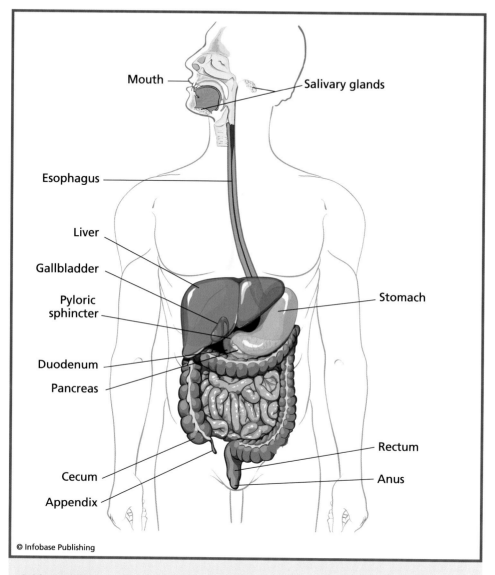

Mouth

Salivary glands

Esophagus

Liver

Gallbladder

Pyloric
sphincter

Stomach

Duodenum

Pancreas

Rectum

Cecum

Anus

Appendix

© Infobase Publishing

Acids and bases exist in the human body and are necessary for its proper function, including the function of the digestion process. When food is swallowed, it is attacked by stomach acids. The stomach acids need to be neutralized before food can continue down the digestive tract. A hormone called secretin monitors the pH balance in the small intestine and sends chemical signals to other parts of the body, thereby regulating pH balance.

Bicarbonate is only one of the digestive chemicals that get secreted into the small intestines. Bile acids play a role as well. Bile is made in the liver, stored in the gallbladder, and, when needed, secreted into the small intestines via the bile duct. Bile plays an essential role in the breakdown of fat by dissolving it in the small intestine, much like soap dissolves oil on a frying pan. This breaks the fat down into small droplets. These fat droplets are broken down even further by other intestinal enzymes so that they can be absorbed by the body.

HOW ACIDS LOWER CHOLESTEROL

Despite the bad press, the body needs cholesterol. In fact, cholesterol is a key ingredient in bile. The more bile the body makes, the lower the amount of cholesterol in the bloodstream.

Pectin, the substance that makes jellies and jams so jelly-like, can help lower blood cholesterol levels by forcing the body to make more bile acids. Pectin is a type of fiber, and like most fiber, pectin cannot be digested by the human body. Instead, the fiber moves slowly through the small intestines. When pectin encounters sugar and acid, its molecules trap water within its long chains, turning into a gel-like mass. This gel traps and eventually eliminates bile acids from the gut. When this happens, the body must make more bile acids, reducing the amount of cholesterol in the blood.

Pectin is found in apples and in the white membrane that surrounds the sections of oranges, grapefruits, or other citrus fruits, as well as in several other sources. Powdered pectin made from apple cores is also available, but scientists have found that eating apples or citrus fruit has a much better effect on lowering blood cholesterol levels than eating powered pectin does. They believe eating the whole fruit is better because the body also needs vitamin C to convert cholesterol into bile acids. Fruits contain vitamin C, or ascorbic acid, but the powdered pectin does not.

BLOOD CHEMISTRY

The normal pH range for the human body is slightly alkaline. On average, the body's pH stays between 7.35 and 7.45. A pH higher than 7.8 or lower than 6.8 is potentially fatal. The body regulates its pH by using **buffers**. Buffers are solutions that resist changes in pH when small amounts of an acid or an alkali are added to the solution. A buffering solution is made up of a weak acid and its salt or a weak base and its salt.

For example, a buffering solution can be made from ethanoic acid (CH_3COOH) and its salt sodium ethanoate (CH_3COONa). Sodium ethanoate completely ionizes in water to form sodium ions and ethanoate ions:

$$CH_3COONa \text{ (aq)} \rightarrow Na^+ \text{ (aq)} + CH_3COO^- \text{ (aq)}$$

sodium ethanoate   sodium ion   ethanoate ion

To make a buffering solution, ethanoic acid is added to the dissolved sodium ethanoate. Because the ethanoic acid is a weak acid, it does not ionize completely. However, it does release hydrogen ions, some of which react with the ethanoate ions to form more ethanoic acid. The solution now contains a lot of ethanoate ions and enough hydrogen ions to make it acidic.

$$CH_3COOH \text{ (aq)} \rightarrow CH_3COO^- \text{ (aq)} + H^+ \text{ (aq)}$$

ethanoic acid   ethanoate ion   hydrogen ion

If an acid is added to this solution, more ethanoic acid is formed. The pH does not change very much because the hydrogen ions introduced by the new acid are soaked up by the ethanoate ions, and the ethanoic acid ionizes only a small amount.

If a base is added to this solution, the hydrogen ions react with the hydroxide ions to form water. If there are hydroxide ions left over, more ethanoic acid breaks down. Again, because most of the introduced hydroxide ions are removed from the solution, the pH does not change very much.

If more and more acid is added, however, the pH will eventually change. Once all the ethanoate ions have been converted to ethanoic acid, an excess of hydrogen ions will build up, leading to a more acidic solution. Likewise, if too much base is added, the ethanoic acid will be used up and excess hydroxide ions will raise the pH. The amount of acid or base that can be added to a buffering solution before the pH changes significantly is called the solution's **buffer capacity**.

In the human body, carbon dioxide provides the buffer. This is called the carbonic acid-hydrogen carbonate ion buffer system. This buffer system maintains the body's blood pH within acceptable levels. The main threat to the blood's pH is excess hydrogen ions produced by various chemical reactions in the body. When hydrogen ions are produced, hydrogen carbonate ions in the blood pick them up and convert them to carbonic acid:

$$HCO_3^- \text{ (aq)} \ + \ H^+ \text{ (aq)} \ \longrightarrow \ H_2CO_3 \text{ (aq)}$$

hydrogen   hydrogen ion   carbonic acid
carbonate ion
(bicarbonate)

When carbonic acid levels become too high, the body releases an enzyme called carbonic anhydrase, which catalyzes the breakdown of carbonic acid into carbon dioxide and water:

$$\overset{\text{enzyme}}{H_2CO_3 \ \rightleftarrows \ CO_2 \ + \ H_2O}$$

carbonic   carbon   water
acid   dioxide

To keep the blood's pH in the acceptable range, the lungs regulate the amount of carbon dioxide in the blood and the kidneys regulate the amount of bicarbonate.

ACIDOSIS

If the body is unable to neutralize acids due to a disease or other problem, a condition called acidosis can result. Acidosis occurs when the blood's pH goes below its normal level of 7.35. One disease that can cause acidosis is diabetes. Diabetic acidosis is caused by a lack of insulin. This condition most often occurs when a Type I diabetic misses his or her scheduled dose of insulin.

Insulin regulates the amount of glucose (a sugar) in the blood. When the body does not have enough insulin, blood sugar levels go up. The body also starts burning fat in an uncontrolled manner.

pH AND HAIR CARE

Normal hair is slightly acidic. In fact, the pH of hair is between 4.5 and 5.5. Hair that becomes too alkaline dries out, tangles easily, becomes dull, and generally looks damaged. Chemical processes, such as permanent waves, hair coloring, and bleaching, as well as a person's natural body chemistry, can all raise the hair's pH.

In an alkaline solution, the cuticle—the outermost layer of a strand of hair—swells up, softens, and becomes rougher. The cuticle is made up of translucent, flattened cells that line the hair shaft like shingles on a roof. The cuticle gets rougher when the cells do not lay flat. When the raised cuticle cells of one piece of hair get stuck on the raised cuticle cells of another piece of hair, the hair tangles. The raised cells also reflect light differently than smooth, flat cells, making the hair appear dull.

Therefore, most shampoos and conditioners are slightly acidic. In acidic solutions, the cuticle shrinks and hardens. This smoothes the raised cuticle cells and causes them to lie flatter. Smooth cuticle cells lead to hair that is less tangled and shinier.

This breakdown of fat creates byproducts, chemicals called ketones. Ketones are acidic. Without enough insulin, they begin to build up in the blood. When enough ketones build up, the blood can no longer buffer the acidity.

Because ketones are passed out of the body in the urine, a doctor can detect the onset of diabetic acidosis by doing a urine test. If ketones are present in the urine, it is a signal to the doctor that the patient's diabetes is out of control. Without treatment, the patient could get very sick. On rare occasions, even Type I or Type II diabetics who take their medication can develop acidosis, usually as a result of some other serious health issue such as an infection or a heart attack.

Diabetic acidosis can develop in a matter of hours. Therefore, under certain circumstances, doctors may ask a diabetic patient to test for ketones at home using special test strips that can detect ketones in urine. For example, doctors recommend that diabetic patients test their urine every 4 to 6 hours if their blood sugar levels are very high. Patients should also test for ketones if they are sick with a cold or the flu, or if they experience any of the symptoms of acidosis. These symptoms include a very dry mouth, frequent urination, shortness of breath, and fruity smelling breath. Diabetic acidosis can be life-threatening, leading to a diabetic coma or death. It needs immediate medical care. Diabetic acidosis is also called ketoacidosis.

Like ketoacidosis, respiratory acidosis can also upset the acid-base balance in the body. Respiratory acidosis occurs when the lungs cannot remove enough carbon dioxide from the body. This may be due to severe lung diseases such as chronic asthma, emphysema, or bronchitis, or it could be caused by mechanical restrictions to the emptying of the lung due to scoliosis (curvature of the spine) or severe obesity.

There are two types of respiratory acidosis. One type, called chronic respiratory acidosis, forms over a long period of time. The body can adjust to this type of respiratory acidosis by signaling the kidneys to produce more bicarbonate. This brings the body's acid-base concentrations back into balance. Acute respiratory acidosis, on the other hand, develops rapidly. The kidneys are unable to react fast enough to keep the blood pH from dropping when the condition develops. Symptoms include confusion, fatigue, and shortness of breath. Like diabetic acidosis, acute respiratory acidosis can be life-threatening, and medical attention is needed immediately.

The blood can also become too alkaline. This condition is called alkalosis. Alkalosis develops when too much carbon dioxide is expelled from the body. The most common cause of this condition is hyperventilation.

LACTIC ACID AND EXERCISE

Sometimes, scientists just get it wrong. That certainly seems to be the case with lactic acid and exercise. For more than a century, lactic acid was seen as the "bad boy" of exercise. People believed that intense, unaccustomed exercise made lactic acid build up in muscles and made them burn and eventually tire and give out. Some athletes even went as far as to have the lactic acid level in their blood tested. Everyone considered lactic acid a toxic waste product. As it turns out, that is not true.

In fact, the muscles use lactic acid (which should actually be called lactate, but people use the two terms interchangeably) as a fuel. Muscles cells make lactic acid on purpose. Scientists have found that cells convert blood glucose into lactic acid. The lactic acid is taken up by mitochondria in muscle cells and burned as fuel. Athletes can exercise with more intensity and for longer periods than most people not because they break down lactic acid faster, as previously thought, but because their muscles contain more mitochondria that absorb more lactic acid, allowing the muscles to produce more energy.

OTHER ACIDS IN THE BODY

Along with stomach, bile, and lactic acids, there are many other acids in the human body. These include, but are not limited to, nucleic acids, amino acids, fatty acids, and vitamins such as folic and ascorbic acids. Nucleic acids, including RNA (ribonucleic acid) and DNA (deoxyribonucleic acid), are long chains of phosphates and sugar to which nucleotide bases are attached. The phosphate molecules in the backbone of RNA and DNA are derived from phosphoric acid. Therefore, DNA is very weakly acidic.

According to Lewis's definition of an acid, that means that DNA is capable of accepting electrons. Unfortunately for the human body, DNA often accepts electrons from oxygen. Certainly the human body needs oxygen to live, but, under certain circumstances, oxygen can also have a harmful effect on the body.

Oxygen is delivered to the cells via the bloodstream. Once in cells, it takes part in the breakdown of glucose. This breakdown produces carbon dioxide and water. In the process, the reaction also releases energy. Oxygen breaks down the glucose molecule by disrupting the chemical bonds that hold it together. It does this by taking an electron away from the glucose molecule, destroying the "glue" that holds the molecule together.

Scientists call an oxygen atom with an extra electron a free radical. The oxygen atom is not stable this way, and it is highly reactive. Because DNA, fats, and proteins are acidic in nature, they are more than willing to take the extra electron from oxygen. Unfortunately, when these substances react with oxygen, their chemical nature changes and they no longer function properly. When cholesterol reacts with oxygen, for example, it changes to the "bad" LDL (low-density lipoprotein) cholesterol that can damage arteries. When proteins in the skin react with a free radical, they lose their elasticity, and the skin wrinkles. DNA that is damaged by free radicals does not replicate like it should, and cancer can result.

Free radicals can cause a lot of damage in the body. Vitamin C, vitamin E, and beta-carotene are known as antioxidants. All of

Antioxidants are found in fruit and vegetables, making them important to eat every day. Antioxidants react with potentially harmful free radicals before the free radicals can react with other molecules in the body.

these compounds react with the free radicals before the free radicals can react with other molecules, such as DNA, fats, and proteins. The antioxidant content of fruits and vegetables is one reason doctors urge people to eat plenty of these foods every day.

Speaking of food that is good for the body, scientists have also found an acid (called docosahexaenoic acid, or DHA) present in fish that they believe plays a very important role in the way the brain functions. DHA is an omega-3 fatty acid. About 60% of the human brain is made up of fat, and most of that appears to be DHA fat.

Low levels of DHA in the blood have been linked to dyslexia, attention deficit disorder, and hyperactivity. They have also been linked to dementia, including Alzheimer's, in the elderly. Scientists have found that these conditions are much less prevalent in cul-

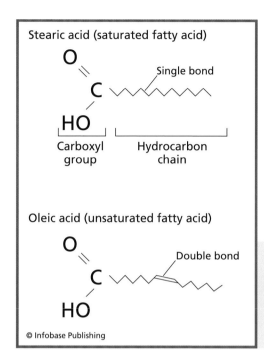

Stearic acid (saturated fatty acid)

Single bond

Carboxyl group

Hydrocarbon chain

Oleic acid (unsaturated fatty acid)

Double bond

© Infobase Publishing

Fatty acids contain a carboxyl group. The carboxyl group gives them their acidic nature.

tures where fish is eaten on a regular basis. Clearly, the brain needs dietary DHA to remain healthy. But what if you do not like fish? Well, you are not completely out of luck: DHA can also be found in eggs and organ meats such as liver.

Fatty acids, like DHA, are the byproducts of the breakdown of fats. DHA and other fatty acids are organic acids. Organic compounds are chemical compounds that contain carbon. Many organic acids in the body contain a -COOH group, called a carboxyl group. The simplest organic acid is methanoic acid (HCOOH). Methanoic acid is also called formic acid. Acetic acid (CH_3COOH) is an organic acid, too. The scientific name for acetic acid is ethanoic acid. In organic chemical nomenclature, the prefix *meth-* means that a compound contains one carbon atom. The prefix *eth-* means the compound has two carbon atoms. Fatty acids contain a carboxyl group, which gives them their acidic nature. Likewise, amino acids are made up of a carboxyl group and an amine group ($-NH_2$). The carboxyl group gives them their acidic nature. Many vitamins, including vitamin C (ascorbic acid), vitamin B_5 (pantothenic acid), B_9 (folic acid), and vitamin A (retinoic acid), also contain carboxyl groups. Organic acids are generally weak acids.

ACID-BASE MEDICATIONS

Sometimes, the body needs some help regulating its acid-base balance. People who experience heartburn, for example, may resort to taking an antacid to neutralize the stomach acid creeping up their esophagus. One popular antacid, milk of magnesia, is actually magnesium hydroxide. The reaction between stomach acid and milk of magnesia is a neutralization reaction:

$$HCl \quad + \quad Mg(OH)_2 \quad \rightarrow \quad MgCl_2 \quad + \quad H_2O$$

stomach	milk of	magnesium	water
acid	magnesia	chloride	
	(an antacid)	(a salt)	

Another common medication, aspirin, is an acid as well. The chemical name for aspirin is acetylsalicylic acid. Aspirin is an organic acid. It contains a carboxyl group and, just like fatty acids and amino acids, the carboxyl group makes the substance weakly acidic. Adding an acidic medication to an already acidic stomach, however, can cause stomach problems. Buffered aspirin is aspirin that has been altered so it does not cause stomach irritation.

Acids and Bases in Nature

Acids and bases are found throughout nature. In fact, acids and bases are used as a defense mechanism by insects and can produce beautiful limestone cave formations. If not monitored carefully, however, acids and bases in the environment can cause a lot of harm.

INSECT VENOM

Many insects use acids and bases to defend themselves from predators. The venom from bee stings, for example, is acidic. Therefore, it would seem reasonable to try to neutralize a bee sting with baking soda. Unfortunately, it is not quite that simple. Bee venom does contain formic acid (also called methanoic acid). If bees only injected the formic acid on top of the skin, baking soda might do a good job of neutralizing the venom's effects. Bees, however, mostly inject their venom in places where baking soda cannot reach. Also, formic acid is only one of the chemicals that causes a bee sting to hurt. In fact, bee venom is made up of 63 different chemicals. There have been a number of reports, however, that a paste of baking soda helps reduce the pain of a bee sting in some people. Baking soda is pretty harmless, so smearing it on the sting site probably will not hurt anything and might be worth a try, anyway.

On the other hand, putting baking soda on a wasp sting would, theoretically, only worsen the pain because wasp stings are basic. Therefore, to soothe a wasp sting, it would make sense to apply an acid like vinegar. Like bee stings, however, there is no scientific evidence to support the idea that vinegar will relieve the pain of a wasp sting. The only things that do seem to work without question are putting ice on the site of the sting (to reduce swelling) and applying a cream that has a combination of an antihistamine (to reduce symptoms of an allergic reaction), an analgesic (to deaden the pain), and a corticosteroid (to reduce swelling).

Other insects besides bees rely on formic acid for defense. Ants use it, too. One particular Amazonian rainforest ant species uses formic acid to secure nesting places for the ant colony. Locals call the places where these ants nest "devil's gardens" because they consist almost entirely of only one type of tree, *Duroia hirsuta*. The Amazonian rainforest has the largest collection of animal and plant species in the world, and most areas have a remarkable variety of trees, shrubs, flowers, and vines. So, an area that has only one species of tree is a little spooky. Local people were convinced that these devil's gardens were planted and tended by evil spirits. In reality, scientists have found that an ant, *Myrmelachista schumanni*, also called the lemon ant, is actually responsible for these patches of homogenous trees. These ants only nest in *D. hirsuta* trees, which are also called, not surprisingly, lemon ant trees. These ant colonies can live for more than 800 years, so abundant nesting areas are essential. The ants make sure that they have plenty of places to nest by poisoning all other plants in the area. Whenever a worker ant

Many insects, like bees, use acids and bases to defend themselves. A bee sting's venom is acidic.

detects a young plant that is not a lemon ant tree, it springs into action and injects formic acid into the leaves of the unwanted plant. Within 24 hours, the invading plant starts to die. This symbiotic relationship between the lemon ant and the lemon ant tree seems to be beneficial to both species.

Other ant species also use formic acid as a weapon. In fact, this acid is fairly common in ants. It got its name from the Latin word *formica*, which means "ant." Some ants, such as the red ant, inject formic acid into their victims just as bees do. Ants, bees, and wasps actually all belong to the same biological order, Hymenoptera. Animals in this order have an ovipositor (a special organ for depositing eggs in hard to reach places). In some ants, bees, and wasps, this ovipositor has evolved into a stinger that is used to inject venom instead of eggs.

Other ants, like the carpenter ant, are incapable of stinging, but that does not stop them from biting and then squirting formic acid into the wound. In this case, because the venom is not injected, a baking soda paste can quickly neutralize the venom and ease the pain. Fire ants, however, have toxic alkaloid venom. Regardless of whether the ant that bites or stings you has acidic or alkaline venom, however, one thing remains the same—it hurts!

Other living things besides animals also use acid to sting. The stinging nettle bush has sharp, hollow hairs that contain various chemicals, including formic acid, that irritate the skin of any animal that is unfortunate enough to rub up against it.

A severe allergic reaction to any of these stinging critters and plants should not be taken lightly. If a person is stung by an ant, bee, or wasp and feels lightheaded, has tightness in their chest, or starts wheezing, they need to be transported to the hospital as quickly as possible. They may be developing a life-threatening allergic reaction to the insect venom.

LIMESTONE CAVE FORMATIONS

The reaction between acids and bases is also responsible for some of the most spectacular, breathtaking cavern formations on Earth. As rainwater falls through the air, it encounters carbon dioxide (CO_2) gas. As it moves through the ground, the rainwater comes into contact with even more carbon dioxide from decaying plants and animals. Eventually, some portion of the rainwater reacts with the carbon dioxide it comes into contact with to form a weak carbonic acid:

$$H_2O \ + \ CO_2 \ \rightarrow \ H_2CO_3$$

water   carbon   carbonic

dioxide   acid

This carbonic acid then comes into contact with limestone beneath the earth. Remember that limestone, a common type of rock, is

Cave formations are caused when rainwater and carbon dioxide mix and form a weak carbonic acid, which then dissolves the calcium carbonate of limestone beneath the earth, allowing for cave formation. The photo shows stalactites and stalagmites and other formations at Luray Caverns in Virginia.

made up of calcium carbonate ($CaCO_3$). Carbonic acid dissolves calcium carbonate. As more and more limestone dissolves, large joints, tunnels, and even caves can form. Because they are formed by dissolving limestone, limestone caves are also called solution caves. This is a form of chemical erosion.

The formations inside limestone caves are made up of limestone, too. Water that drains through the cracks in rock and into a limestone cave often contains dissolved limestone. As the drop of water hangs from the ceiling, some of the carbon dioxide trapped in the water escapes. When this occurs, the water can no longer hold as much dissolved limestone as it did before. Therefore, some limestone, which is now a solid, is deposited on the ceiling. This process continues, drop after drop, until a stalactite forms. Stalactite formation is an extremely slow process. In fact, stalactites only grow about one-half an inch every 100 years.

ATTACK OF THE ACIDS

Bees and ants are not the only critters that attack using acid. Bacteria, such as those found in plaque, do, too. Saliva usually keeps the mouth at a pH of about 6.8. Any pH of 6.0 or higher does not cause the teeth any problems. Plaque, a bacteria-containing film that builds up on teeth, can cause that pH to plummet. That is because it contains bacteria such as *Streptococcus mutans*, *Lactobacillus casei*, and *Lactobacillus acidophilus* that feed on sugars and make lactic acid. These conditions can lower the pH in the mouth to 5.5 or less.

Under these acidic conditions, tooth enamel starts to break down, leading to dental caries (or cavities). When *S. mutans*, *L. casei*, and *L. acidophilus* are around, it does not matter how much sugar is in food or drinks. What really matters is how long the sugar is in contact with the acid-producing bacteria on the teeth. The longer the bacteria and the sugar are in contact, the more acid is produced. Acids in soft drinks, tea, and citrus drinks do not help either. The best way to return the mouth to a neutral pH is to brush your teeth, especially with toothpaste that contains fluoride. Fluoride, found in tap water as well as toothpaste, strengthens the tooth enamel. Stronger enamel is less susceptible to the damage caused by the lactic acid produced by the bacteria.

Stalagmites are cave formations that start on the floor and grow upward. These formations are caused when water that contains dissolved limestone drips from the ceiling of the cave and lands on the same spot. Sometimes, water dripping off of a stalactite will actually form a stalagmite directly below it. Eventually, a column forms when the stalactite and stalagmite meet. This feature can take thousands or even millions of years to form.

FOOD PROCESSING AND FLAVORING

Bacteria not only attack teeth but can also make people extremely sick. Therefore, canned food must be specially prepared to prevent the growth of bacteria. This is usually done by boiling or steaming. People who can their own food at home, however, do not have the sophisticated machines that food-canning manufacturers have. Even so, there are other methods that home canners can use to preserve their own food and keep their families safe. For example, high heat can be used to kill the bacteria *Clostridium botulinum,* which causes one deadly form of food poisoning called botulism. Acidic conditions will also kill *C. botulinum.* Because the bacteria cannot survive at a pH below 4.5, very acidic foods such as tomatoes, pears, and peaches are safe for home canning.

Foods such as cucumbers and cabbage, however, are not acidic enough to be safe. Cucumbers can be preserved safely by placing them in a salt and vinegar solution. This process, called pickling, is the method used to make pickles from cucumbers. The vinegar in the pickling solution drops the acidity of the cucumbers to about 3.0 so they can safely be consumed. To keep cabbage, many people ferment the cabbage into sauerkraut. Sauerkraut's pH is about 3.7.

ACIDS AND BASES IN THE ENVIRONMENT

Venus is not the only planet in the solar system that has sulfuric acid in its atmosphere. Earth has it, too. Unlike Venus, where the surface temperatures are too hot for acidic rain to reach the ground, the Earth does not enjoy that same protection. Therefore, acid rain can be a serious problem on this, the third rock from the Sun.

ACIDS AND BASES DO NOT MIX

When acids and bases are mixed, a neutralization reaction occurs. Not all acids and bases should be mixed, however. Bleach, which is a solution of sodium or calcium hypochlorite, for example, should never be mixed with any kind of acid because the resulting chemical reaction creates the deadly gas chlorine. Chlorine gas was used as a chemical weapon in World War I, and breathing it can destroy lung tissue. The lungs fill with fluid, and the unfortunate victim eventually dies by suffocation.

Read the labels before mixing household cleansers. Many toilet-bowl cleaners contain acidic solutions, as do some drain cleaners, rust removers, and, of course, vinegar. Never mix bleach with these products. You could sustain permanent lung damage.

While some drain cleaners contain concentrated sulfuric acid, many more contain sodium hydroxide. Mixing these two chemicals will not release chlorine gas, but the reaction between them does release a great amount of heat. Someone who makes the mistake of trying to unclog their sink with one product and then switches to a different drain cleaner when the first does not clear the drain fast enough could create enough steam to blast the whole corrosive mess out of the sink right into their face.

Ammonia and chlorine bleach should never be mixed either. Even though bleach and ammonia are both bases, they still give off chloramine (NH_2Cl) vapor when they are mixed. Chloramine is not as dangerous as chlorine gas, but it can be irritating to respiratory passages in large quantities. The chlorine that is added to swimming pools often comes in the form of sodium hypochlorate, the same active ingredient as in household bleach. The smell of chlorine that hangs around the swimming pool is not chlorine gas, but comes from chloramines, along with other compounds, that are formed when the chlorine used to sanitize the pool comes into contact with urea, a component of urine. How the urea got into the water to begin with is an entirely different story.

Acid rain occurs when water comes into contact with sulfur and nitrogen oxides in the atmosphere, which can come from natural sources or from man-made sources like cars or power plants. These acid rain-damaged coniferous trees live in the Karkonosze National Park in Silesia, Poland.

Acid rain is actually a catchall phrase for any kind of acidic precipitation, including snow, sleet, mist, and fog. Acid rain begins when water comes into contact with sulfur and nitrogen oxides in the atmosphere. These oxides can come from natural sources such as volcanic emissions or decaying plants. But there are man-made sources as well, such as power plant and automobile emissions. In the United States, two-thirds of all the sulfur dioxide and one-fourth of the nitrogen oxides in the atmosphere are produced by coal-burning power plants.

When water comes into contact with a sulfur oxide, such as sulfur dioxide, sulfuric acid is formed just like it is in Venus' atmosphere or in a sulfuric acid manufacturing plant. Nitric and nitrous acids are formed when nitrogen dioxide reacts with water:

$$2\ NO_2\ +\ H_2O\ \rightarrow\ HNO_3\ +\ HNO_2$$

| nitrogen | water | nitric | nitrous |
| dioxide | | acid | acid |

Acid precipitation can contain any of these acids.

The low pH of acid precipitation can destroy forests and kill fish. Some lakes and streams lie in soil that has the natural ability to buffer the increased acidity of acid rain, usually because the soil contains a high amount of lime. Other lakes and streams, however, have no such buffering capacity. The pH of the water is not the main problem—at least not directly. The problem lies in the amount of aluminum compounds that are leached out of the soil surrounding the lake or stream at lower pHs. Aluminum is toxic to many aquatic species.

Ideally, lakes and streams have a pH between 6 and 8. However, according to the National Surface Water Survey (NSWS) conducted by the U.S. Environmental Protection Agency between 1984 and 1986, the most acidic lake in the country, Little Echo Pond in Franklin, New York, had a pH of 4.2. According to the same survey, the Pine Barrens region of New Jersey also has a very high percentage of acidic rivers. More than 90% of the streams in that area are considered acidic. This is very bad news for the fish that live in these lakes and streams.

Many lakes also suffer from a phenomenon called episodic acidity. Episodic acidity means that most of the time the lake has a pH within acceptable levels. But occasionally, the pH of the lake becomes much lower when heavy rainstorms or snow melts bring in large amounts of runoff. Episodic acidity sometimes results in large fish kills. The Northeastern part of the United States and Canada are especially hard hit due to the poor buffering capacity of the soil in those areas.

	pH 6.5	pH 6.0	pH 5.5	pH 5.0	pH 4.5	pH 4.0
Snails						
Clams						
Bass						
Crayfish						
Mayfly						
Trout						
Salamanders						
Perch						
Frogs						

Source: Environmental Protection Agency
© Infobase Publishing

Low pH levels can kill living aquatic animals and prevent their eggs from hatching. The above diagram shows which pH levels kill which type of water-dwelling creature.

Not only can a low pH kill living fish, but also it can prevent fish eggs from hatching at all. In fact, most fish eggs will not hatch below a pH of 5. Adult fish and shellfish, however, die at differing pHs. Clams and snails, for example, cannot withstand a pH much lower than 6. Crayfish, bass, and mayflies (insects eaten by many fish) disappear when the pH falls below 5.5. Trout, perch, salamanders, and frogs can survive in slightly more acidic water. At a pH of 4, frogs can withstand the most acidic conditions. Unfortunately for the frogs, however, their main food supply, mayflies, drops out at a pH of 5.5.

In areas where lakes are particularly acidic, people have tried to neutralize the acid in the lakes by adding powdered lime (calcium oxide). Making a lake too alkaline, however, can be equally harmful to aquatic plants and animals, and determining the safe amount of lime to add is a difficult problem.

Acid rain not only harms plants and animals, but also it can destroy buildings and statues. Limestone and marble, common building materials, are easily dissolved by acids. Try this: Put a drop of vinegar on a piece of chalk. Notice how the chalk fizzes and dissolves when exposed to the acetic acid in vinegar. That is because chalk, like limestone and marble, is mainly composed of calcium carbonate:

$$CaCO_3 \ + \ HC_2H_3O_2 \ \rightarrow \ Ca(C_2H_3O_2)_2 \ + \ CO_2 \ (g) \ + \ H_2O$$

calcium	acetic	calcium	carbon	water
carbonate	acid	acetate	dioxide	
(chalk)	(vinegar)		(gas)	

Bubbles of carbon dioxide gas form when the vinegar hits the chalk. A piece of chalk covered in vinegar and left for a couple of days will completely dissolve. Limestone rocks dissolve in carbonic acid to form limestone caves, and marble buildings and statues will eventually dissolve in acidic rain, too.

The best way to prevent these problems is to prevent acid rain at the start. Reducing emissions from automobiles and power plants would help reduce acid-rain levels. This means conserving energy and driving less. The less energy people use, the less coal needs to be burned to produce electricity. These measures help decrease the sulfur and nitrogen oxides in the atmosphere and, therefore, decrease the amount of acid rain.

Aside from the environmental problems they can cause, acids and bases play an extremely important role in our ordinary, everyday lives. Acids and bases can also be dangerous. They must be handled with care. Knowing a little bit about acid-base chemistry can help citizens understand the benefits and dangers of these chemicals. Informed citizens can then make intelligent decisions about industrial processes and any future actions, such as legislation, that may be needed to control these important and beneficial chemicals.

PERIODIC TABLE OF THE ELEMENTS

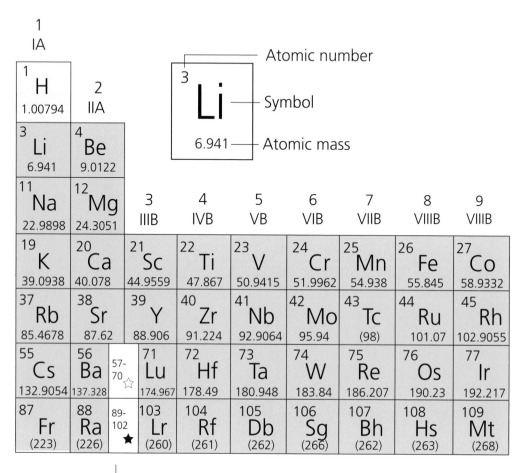

1 IA								
1 **H** 1.00794	2 IIA							
3 **Li** 6.941	4 **Be** 9.0122	3 IIIB	4 IVB	5 VB	6 VIB	7 VIIB	8 VIIIB	9 VIIIB
11 **Na** 22.9898	12 **Mg** 24.3051							
19 **K** 39.0938	20 **Ca** 40.078	21 **Sc** 44.9559	22 **Ti** 47.867	23 **V** 50.9415	24 **Cr** 51.9962	25 **Mn** 54.938	26 **Fe** 55.845	27 **Co** 58.9332
37 **Rb** 85.4678	38 **Sr** 87.62	39 **Y** 88.906	40 **Zr** 91.224	41 **Nb** 92.9064	42 **Mo** 95.94	43 **Tc** (98)	44 **Ru** 101.07	45 **Rh** 102.9055
55 **Cs** 132.9054	56 **Ba** 137.328	57-70 ☆	71 **Lu** 174.967	72 **Hf** 178.49	73 **Ta** 180.948	74 **W** 183.84	75 **Re** 186.207	76 **Os** 190.23	77 **Ir** 192.217
87 **Fr** (223)	88 **Ra** (226)	89-102 ★	103 **Lr** (260)	104 **Rf** (261)	105 **Db** (262)	106 **Sg** (266)	107 **Bh** (262)	108 **Hs** (263)	109 **Mt** (268)

Atomic number
3
Li
Symbol
6.941 — Atomic mass

☆ Lanthanoids

★ Actinoids

57 **La** 138.9055	58 **Ce** 140.115	59 **Pr** 140.908	60 **Nd** 144.24	61 **Pm** (145)
89 **Ac** (227)	90 **Th** 232.0381	91 **Pa** 231.036	92 **U** 238.0289	93 **Np** (237)

Numbers in parentheses are atomic mass numbers of most stable isotopes.

Metals

Non-metals

Metalloids

Unknown

			13 IIIA	14 IVA	15 VA	16 VIA	17 VIIA	18 VIIIA
								2 He 4.0026
			5 B 10.81	6 C 12.011	7 N 14.0067	8 O 15.9994	9 F 18.9984	10 Ne 20.1798
10 VIIIB	11 IB	12 IIB	13 Al 26.9815	14 Si 28.0855	15 P 30.9738	16 S 32.067	17 Cl 35.4528	18 Ar 39.948
28 Ni 58.6934	29 Cu 63.546	30 Zn 65.409	31 Ga 69.723	32 Ge 72.61	33 As 74.9216	34 Se 78.96	35 Br 79.904	36 Kr 83.798
46 Pd 106.42	47 Ag 107.8682	48 Cd 112.412	49 In 114.818	50 Sn 118.711	51 Sb 121.760	52 Te 127.60	53 I 126.9045	54 Xe 131.29
78 Pt 195.08	79 Au 196.9655	80 Hg 200.59	81 Tl 204.3833	82 Pb 207.2	83 Bi 208.9804	84 Po (209)	85 At (210)	86 Rn (222)
110 Ds (271)	111 Rg (272)	112 Uub (277)	113 Uut (284)	114 Uuq (285)	115 Uup (288)	116 Uuh (292)	117 Uus ?	118 Uuo ?

62 Sm 150.36	63 Eu 151.966	64 Gd 157.25	65 Tb 158.9253	66 Dy 162.500	67 Ho 164.9303	68 Er 167.26	69 Tm 168.9342	70 Yb 173.04
94 Pu (244)	95 Am 243	96 Cm (247)	97 Bk (247)	98 Cf (251)	99 Es (252)	100 Fm (257)	101 Md (258)	102 No (259)

ELECTRON CONFIGURATIONS

1
IA
ns^1

Atomic number

3
Li

[He] $2s^1$ — Symbol / Electron configuration

1	2							
1 H $1s^1$	ns²							
3 Li [He]$2s^1$	**4** Be [He]$2s^2$							

		3 IIIB	4 IVB	5 VB	6 VIB	7 VIIB	8 VIIIB	9 VIIIB
11 Na [Ne]$3s^1$	**12** Mg [Ne]$3s^2$							
19 K [Ar]$4s^1$	**20** Ca [Ar] $4s^2$	**21** Sc [Ar]$4s^23d^1$	**22** Ti [Ar]$4s^23d^2$	**23** V [Ar]$4s^23d^3$	**24** Cr [Ar]$4s^13d^5$	**25** Mn [Ar]$4s^23d^5$	**26** Fe [Ar]$4s^23d^6$	**27** Co [Ar]$4s^23d^7$
37 Rb [Kr]$5s^1$	**38** Sr [Kr]$5s^2$	**39** Y [Kr]$5s^24d^1$	**40** Zr [Kr]$5s^24d^2$	**41** Nb [Kr]$5s^14d^4$	**42** Mo [Kr]$5s^14d^5$	**43** Tc [Kr]$5s^14d^6$	**44** Ru [Kr]$5s^14d^7$	**45** Rh [Kr]$5s^14d^8$
55 Cs [Xe]$6s^1$	**56** Ba [Xe]$6s^2$	57-70 ☆	**71** Lu [Xe]$6s^24f^{14}5d^1$	**72** Hf [Xe]$4f^{14}6s^25d^2$	**73** Ta [Xe]$6s^25d^3$	**74** W [Xe]$6s^25d^4$	**75** Re [Xe]$6s^25d^5$	**76** Os [Xe]$6s^25d^6$	**77** Ir [Xe]$6s^25d^7$
87 Fr [Rn]$7s^1$	**88** Ra [Rn]$7s^2$	89-102 ★	**103** Lr [Rn]$7s^25f^{14}6d^1$	**104** Rf [Rn]$7s^26d^2$	**105** Db [Rn]$7s^26d^3$	**106** Sg [Rn]$7s^26d^4$	**107** Bh [Rn]$7s^26d^5$	**108** Hs [Rn]$7s^26d^6$	**109** Mt [Rn]$7s^26d^7$

☆ Lanthanoids

★ Actinoids

57 La [Xe] $6s^25d^1$	**58** Ce [Xe] $6s^24f^15d^1$	**59** Pr [Xe] $6s^24f^35d^0$	**60** Nd [Xe] $6s^24f^45d^0$	**61** Pm [Xe] $6s^24f^55d^0$
89 Ac [Rn]$7s^26d^1$	**90** Th [Rn] $7s^25f^06d^2$	**91** Pa [Rn] $7s^25f^26d^1$	**92** U [Rn] $7s^25f^36d^1$	**93** Np [Rn] $7s^25f^46d^1$

									18 VIIIA ns^2np^6
			13 IIIA ns^2np^1	14 IVA ns^2np^2	15 VA ns^2np^3	16 VIA ns^2np^4	17 VIIA ns^2np^5		2 He $1s^2$

10 VIIIB	11 IB	12 IIB	13 IIIA ns^2np^1	14 IVA ns^2np^2	15 VA ns^2np^3	16 VIA ns^2np^4	17 VIIA ns^2np^5	18 VIIIA ns^2np^6
			5 B $[He]2s^22p^1$	6 C $[He]2s^22p^2$	7 N $[He]2s^22p^3$	8 O $[He]2s^22p^4$	9 F $[He]2s^22p^5$	10 Ne $[He]2s^22p^6$
			13 Al $[Ne]3s^23p^1$	14 Si $[Ne]3s^23p^2$	15 P $[Ne]3s^23p^3$	16 S $[Ne]3s^23p^4$	17 Cl $[Ne]3s^23p^5$	18 Ar $[Ne]3s^23p^6$
28 Ni $[Ar]4s^23d^8$	29 Cu $[Ar]4s^13d^{10}$	30 Zn $[Ar]4s^23d^{10}$	31 Ga $[Ar]4s^24p^1$	32 Ge $[Ar]4s^24p^2$	33 As $[Ar]4s^24p^3$	34 Se $[Ar]4s^24p^4$	35 Br $[Ar]4s^24p^5$	36 Kr $[Ar]4s^24p^6$
46 Pd $[Kr]4d^{10}$	47 Ag $[Kr]5s^14d^{10}$	48 Cd $[Kr]5s^24d^{10}$	49 In $[Kr]5s^25p^1$	50 Sn $[Kr]5s^25p^2$	51 Sb $[Kr]5s^25p^3$	52 Te $[Kr]5s^25p^4$	53 I $[Kr]5s^25p^5$	54 Xe $[Kr]5s^25p^6$
78 Pt $[Xe]6s^15d^9$	79 Au $[Xe]6s^15d^{10}$	80 Hg $[Xe]6s^25d^{10}$	81 Tl $[Xe]6s^26p^1$	82 Pb $[Xe]6s^26p^2$	83 Bi $[Xe]6s^26p^3$	84 Po $[Xe]6s^26p^4$	85 At $[Xe]6s^26p^5$	86 Rn $[Xe]6s^26p^6$
110 Ds $[Rn]7s^16d^9$	111 Rg $[Rn]7s^16d^{10}$	112 Uub $[Rn]7s^26d^{10}$	113 Uut ?	114 Uuq ?	115 Uup ?	116 Uuh ?	117 Uus ?	118 Uuo ?

62 Sm [Xe] $6s^24f^65d^0$	63 Eu [Xe] $6s^24f^75d^0$	64 Gd [Xe] $6s^24f^75d^1$	65 Tb [Xe] $6s^24f^95d^0$	66 Dy [Xe] $6s^24f^{10}5d^0$	67 Ho [Xe] $6s^24f^{11}5d^0$	68 Er [Xe] $6s^24f^{12}5d^0$	69 Tm [Xe] $6s^24f^{13}5d^0$	70 Yb [Xe] $6s^24f^{14}5d^0$
94 Pu [Rn] $7s^25f^66d^0$	95 Am [Rn] $7s^25f^76d^0$	96 Cm [Rn] $7s^25f^76d^1$	97 Bk [Rn] $7s^25f^96d^0$	98 Cf [Rn] $7s^25f^{10}6d^0$	99 Es [Rn] $7s^25f^{11}6d^0$	100 Fm [Rn] $7s^25f^{12}6d^0$	101 Md [Rn] $7s^25f^{13}6d^0$	102 No [Rn] $7s^25f^{14}6d^1$

TABLE OF ATOMIC MASSES

ELEMENT	SYMBOL	ATOMIC NUMBER	ATOMIC MASS
Actinium	Ac	89	(227)
Aluminum	Al	13	26.9815
Americium	Am	95	243
Antimony	Sb	51	121.76
Argon	Ar	18	39.948
Arsenic	As	33	74.9216
Astatine	At	85	(210)
Barium	Ba	56	137.328
Berkelium	Bk	97	(247)
Beryllium	Be	4	9.0122
Bismuth	Bi	83	208.9804
Bohrium	Bh	107	(262)
Boron	B	5	10.81
Bromine	Br	35	79.904
Cadmium	Cd	48	112.412
Calcium	Ca	20	40.078
Californium	Cf	98	(251)
Carbon	C	6	12.011
Cerium	Ce	58	140.115
Cesium	Cs	55	132.9054
Chlorine	Cl	17	35.4528
Chromium	Cr	24	51.9962
Cobalt	Co	27	58.9332
Copper	Cu	29	63.546
Curium	Cm	96	(247)
Darmstadtium	Ds	110	(271)
Dubnium	Db	105	(262)
Dysprosium	Dy	66	162.5
Einsteinium	Es	99	(252)
Erbium	Er	68	167.26
Europium	Eu	63	151.966
Fermium	Fm	100	(257)
Fluorine	F	9	18.9984

ELEMENT	SYMBOL	ATOMIC NUMBER	ATOMIC MASS
Francium	Fr	87	(223)
Gadolinium	Gd	64	157.25
Gallium	Ga	31	69.723
Germanium	Ge	32	72.61
Gold	Au	79	196.9655
Hafnium	Hf	72	178.49
Hassium	Hs	108	(263)
Helium	He	2	4.0026
Holmium	Ho	67	164.9303
Hydrogen	H	1	1.00794
Indium	In	49	114.818
Iodine	I	53	126.9045
Iridium	Ir	77	192.217
Iron	Fe	26	55.845
Krypton	Kr	36	83.798
Lanthanum	La	57	138.9055
Lawrencium	Lr	103	(260)
Lead	Pb	82	207.2
Lithium	Li	3	6.941
Lutetium	Lu	71	174.967
Magnesium	Mg	12	24.3051
Manganese	Mn	25	54.938
Meitnerium	Mt	109	(268)
Mendelevium	Md	101	(258)
Mercury	Hg	80	200.59
Molybdenum	Mo	42	95.94
Neodymium	Nd	60	144.24
Neon	Ne	10	20.1798
Neptunium	Np	93	(237)
Nickel	Ni	28	58.6934
Niobium	Nb	41	92.9064
Nitrogen	N	7	14.0067
Nobelium	No	102	(259)

ELEMENT	SYMBOL	ATOMIC NUMBER	ATOMIC MASS
Osmium	Os	76	190.23
Oxygen	O	8	15.9994
Palladium	Pd	46	106.42
Phosphorus	P	15	30.9738
Platinum	Pt	78	195.08
Plutonium	Pu	94	(244)
Polonium	Po	84	(209)
Potassium	K	19	39.0938
Praseodymium	Pr	59	140.908
Promethium	Pm	61	(145)
Protactinium	Pa	91	231.036
Radium	Ra	88	(226)
Radon	Rn	86	(222)
Rhenium	Re	75	186.207
Rhodium	Rh	45	102.9055
Roentgenium	Rg	111	(272)
Rubidium	Rb	37	85.4678
Ruthenium	Ru	44	101.07
Rutherfordium	Rf	104	(261)
Samarium	Sm	62	150.36
Scandium	Sc	21	44.9559
Seaborgium	Sg	106	(266)
Selenium	Se	34	78.96

ELEMENT	SYMBOL	ATOMIC NUMBER	ATOMIC MASS
Silicon	Si	14	28.0855
Silver	Ag	47	107.8682
Sodium	Na	11	22.9898
Strontium	Sr	38	87.62
Sulfur	S	16	32.067
Tantalum	Ta	73	180.948
Technetium	Tc	43	(98)
Tellurium	Te	52	127.6
Terbium	Tb	65	158.9253
Thallium	Tl	81	204.3833
Thorium	Th	90	232.0381
Thulium	Tm	69	168.9342
Tin	Sn	50	118.711
Titanium	Ti	22	47.867
Tungsten	W	74	183.84
Ununbium	Uub	112	(277)
Uranium	U	92	238.0289
Vanadium	V	23	50.9415
Xenon	Xe	54	131.29
Ytterbium	Yb	70	173.04
Yttrium	Y	39	88.906
Zinc	Zn	30	65.409
Zirconium	Zr	40	91.224

GLOSSARY

Acid-base indicator   A substance that changes color in the presence of an acid or a base.

Amphoteric   A compound that can act as an acid or a base depending on the circumstances.

Anion   A negatively charged ion.

Atom   The smallest unit of an element that still has the same properties as the element.

Binary acid   An acid composed of only two elements.

Buffer   A solution that resists a change in pH when small amounts of an acid or an alkali are added.

Buffer capacity   The amount of acid or base that can be added to a buffering solution before the pH changes significantly.

Cation   A positively charged ion.

Compound   Two or more elements chemically bonded together.

Concentrated   Having a high percentage of acid or base as compared to water in a solution.

Conjugate acid   The substance formed when a base accepts a hydrogen ion.

Conjugate base   The substance formed when an acid donates a hydrogen ion.

Dilute   Having a high percentage of water as compared to acid or base in a solution.

Disassociation   To break down into ions.

Double displacement reaction   A chemical reaction in which the positive ion in one reactant takes the place of the positive ion in the other reactant.

Dynamic equilibrium   When the forward reaction and the backward reaction in a reversible reaction occur at the same rate.

Electricity   A flow of electrons.

Electrolyte   A substance that conducts electricity.

Electron   A negatively charged subatomic particle found traveling around the outside of an atom's nucleus in energy levels, or shells.

Element   A substance that cannot be broken down into simpler substances by ordinary chemical means.

Enzyme   A biological catalyst.

Exothermic   A chemical reaction that releases heat.

Heterogeneous   A substance that is not uniform in composition.

Homogenous   A substance uniform in composition.

Ion   A charged particle formed when an atom gains or loses electrons.

Ionic compound   A compound that is made up of positively and negatively charged ions.

Ionization   To break down into ions.

Law of conservation of matter   A law that states that matter can neither be created nor destroyed.

Neutralization reaction   A chemical reaction between an acid and a base that produces a salt and water.

Neutron   A neutral subatomic particle found in the nucleus of an atom.

Nucleus   The center of an atom.

Octet rule   A rule of thumb that states that atoms are in a more stable state when their outermost energy level contains eight electrons.

Polyatomic ion   A charged group of atoms that react as a unit.

Precipitate   A solid that forms in a solution due to a chemical reaction taking place.

Product   A new substance formed in a chemical reaction.

Proton   A positively charged subatomic particle found in the nucleus of an atom.

Reactants   The substances present at the beginning of a chemical reaction.

Salt   An ionic compound formed by the reaction of an acid and a base.

Soluble   When a substance is capable of being dissolved.

Solution   A homogenous mixture of two or more substances.

Strong acid   An acid that completely ionizes in water.

Strong base   A base that completely ionizes in water.

Valence electron   The electrons in the outermost energy level of an atom that are involved in chemical bonding with other atoms.

Weak acid   An acid that does not completely ionize in water.

Weak base   A base that does not completely ionize in water.

BIBLIOGRAPHY

American Chemical Society. "Aqua regia." Available online. URL: http://jchemed.chem.wisc.edu/JCEsoft/CCA/CCA3/MAIN/AQREGIA/PAGE1.HTM. Accessed on January 21, 2008.

American Chemistry Council. "Hydrochloric acid-HCl—an acid with many uses." Available online. URL: http://www.americanchemistry.com/s_chlorine/science_sec.asp?CID=1255&DID=4735&CTYPEID=113. Accessed on March 17, 2008.

American Diabetes Association. "Ketoacidosis." Available online. URL: http://www.diabetes.org/type-1-diabetes/ketoacidosis.jsp. Accessed on March 18, 2008.

American Geophysical Union. "Venusian vignette." Available online. URL: http://www.agu.org/sci_soc/venusian.html. Accessed on March 11, 2008.

Australian Museum. "What is grave wax?" Available online. URL: http://www.deathonline.net/decomposition/body_changes/grave_wax.htm. Accessed on March 11, 2008.

Carpi, Anthony. "Acids and bases: An introduction," *Visionlearning* Vol. CHE-2 (2), 2003. Available online. URL: http://www.visionlearning.com/library/module_viewer.php?mid=58. Accessed on January 21, 2008.

Cobb, Cathy, and Monty L. Fetterolf. *The Joy of Chemistry: The Amazing Science of Familiar Things*. Amherst, N.Y.: Prometheus Books, 2005.

Darling, David. "Kipp's apparatus," The Internet Encyclopedia of Science Web site. Available online. URL: http://www.daviddarling.info/encyclopedia/K/Kipps_apparatus.html. Accessed on March 17, 2008.

Decelles, Paul. "The pH scale," Dr. Paul's Virtually Biology Show Web site. Available online. URL: http://staff.jccc.net/PDECELL/chemistry/phscale.html. Accessed on March 13, 2008.

Deem, James. "Mummification in Egypt," Mummy Tombs Web Site. Available online. URL: http://www.mummytombs.com/egypt/methods.htm. Accessed on March 17, 2008.

Duke University Office of News & Communications. "130-year-old mysteries solved: How nitroglycerin works; why patients develop tolerance," Duke University Web site. Available online. URL: http://www.dukenews.duke.edu/2002/06/nitro0602.html. Accessed on March 11, 2008.

Eggling, Sue. "Reactions," Clackamas Community College Web site. Available online. URL: http://dl.clackamas.cc.or.us/ch106–05/reaction2.htm. Accessed on January 21, 2008.

European Space Agency. "Venus express." Available online. URL: http://www.esa.int/esaMI/Venus_Express/SEMFPY808BE_0.html. Accessed on March 10, 2008.

Jol, Harry. "Cave formations," University of Wisconsin—Eau Claire Web site. Available online. URL: http://www.uwec.edu/jolhm/Cave/caveform2.htm. Accessed on March 19, 2008.

Katz, David. "Bloodstain patterns," Chymist.com Web site. Available online. URL: http://www.chymist.com/BLOODSTAIN%20PATTERNS.pdf. Accessed on March 17, 2008.

Katz, Larry. "Pool water pH," Pool Wizard Web site. Available online. URL: http://www.havuz.org/pool_pool/pool_maintenance/water_testing/ph.htm. Accessed on March 14, 2008.

Kiefer, David. "Soda ash, Solvay style," American Chemical Society Web site. Available online. URL: http://pubs.acs.org/subscribe/journals/tcaw/11/i02/html/02chemchron.html. Accessed on March 17, 2008.

King, Michael. "Biochemistry of amino acids," University of Brescia Web site. Available online. URL: http://www.med.unibs.it/~marchesi/aacids.html. Accessed on March 18, 2008.

Knox, Gary. "French hydrangea for gardens in North and Central Florida," University of Florida, Institute of Food and Agricultural Sciences Web site. Available online. URL: http://edis.ifas. ufl.edu/EP330. Accessed on March 13, 2008.

Kolata, Gina. "Lactic acid is not muscles' foe, it's fuel," *New York Times* Web site. Available online. URL: http://www.nytimes. com/2006/05/16/health/nutrition/16run.html?_r=2&oref= slogin&oref=slogin. Accessed on March 18, 2008.

Merck & Co., Inc. "Bee, wasp, hornet, and ant stings," Merck Web site. Available online. URL: http://www.merck.com/mmhe/ sec24/ch298/ch298g.html. Accessed on March 19, 2008.

Merck & Co., Inc. "Cavities," Merck Web site. Available online. URL: http://www.merck.com/mmhe/sec08/ch114/ch114b.html. Accessed on March 19, 2008.

Murphy, Pat. "Better hair through chemistry," Exploration Web site. Available online. URL: http://www.exploratorium.edu/ exploring/hair/index.html. Accessed on March 18, 2008.

National Digestive Diseases Information Clearinghouse. "Your digestive system and how it works," National Digestive Diseases Information Clearinghouse Web site. Available online. URL: http://digestive.niddk.nih.gov/ddiseases/pubs/yrdd/. Accessed on March 18, 2008.

Nave, Rod. "The atmosphere of Venus," Georgia State University Web site. Available online. URL: http://hyperphysics.phy-astr. gsu.edu/hbase/solar/venusenv.html. Accessed on March 10, 2008.

Nobel Foundation. "Ascanio sobrero," Nobelprize.org. Available online. URL: http://nobelprize.org/alfred_nobel/biographical/ articles/life-work/sobrero.html. Accessed on March 10, 2008.

Nobel Foundation. "Carl Bosch–Biography," Nobelprize.org. Available online. URL: http://nobelprize.org/nobel_prizes/chemistry/ laureates/1931/bosch-bio.html. Accessed on March 17, 2008.

Nobel Foundation. "The Nobel Prize in Chemistry 1918–Presentation Speech," Nobelprize.org. Available online. URL: http://nobelprize.org/nobel_prizes/chemistry/laureates/1918/press.html. Accessed on March 17, 2008.

Nobel Foundation. "The Nobel Prize in Physiology or Medicine 1998," Nobelprize.org. Available online. URL: http://nobelprize.org/nobel_prizes/medicine/laureates/1998/press.html. Accessed on March 11, 2008.

North American Galvanizing. "The hot dip galvanizing process." Available online. URL: http://www.nagalv.com/services_hotdip.asp. Accessed on March 17, 2008.

Oceanus Creative Technologies. "Extinguisher types." Available online. URL: http://www.fireturnkey.com/ext_types.htm. Accessed on March 14, 2008.

Ophardt, Charles. "Neutralization," Elmhurst College Virtual ChemBook Web site. Available online. URL: http://www.elmhurst.edu/~chm/vchembook/183neutral.html. Accessed on March 17, 2008.

Ophardt, Charles. "Respiratory acidosis," Elmhurst College Virtual ChemBook Web site. Available online. URL: http://www.elmhurst.edu/~chm/vchembook/263respiratoryacid.html. Accessed on March 18, 2008.

PBS Online. "Rough science: The challenge: recharge a battery," Rough Science Web site. Available online. URL: http://www.pbs.org/weta/roughscience/series2/challenges/battery/. Accessed on March 17, 2008.

Plambeck, James. "The alkali industry," University of Alberta Web site. Available online. URL: http://www.ualberta.ca/~jplambec/che/p101/p01261.htm. Accessed on March 17, 2008.

Purdue Research Foundation. "Oven cleaner." Available online. URL: http://www.purdue.edu/envirosoft/housewaste/house/ovencl.htm. Accessed on January 21, 2008.

Purdue University School of Veterinary Medicine. "Stinging nettle," Purdue University Web site. Available online. URL: http://www.vet.purdue.edu/depts/addl/toxic/plant31.htm. Accessed on March 19, 2008.

Reusch, William. "Nucleic Acids," Michigan State University Web site. Available online. URL: http://www.cem.msu.edu/~reusch/VirtualText/nucacids.htm. Accessed on March 18, 2008.

Ringertz, Nils. "Alfred Nobel: His Life and Work," Nobelprize.org. Available online. URL: http://nobelprize.org/alfred_nobel/biographical/articles/life-work/index.html. Accessed on March 11, 2008.

Roach, John. "Ants use acid to make 'gardens' in Amazon, study says," *National Geographic* Web site. Available online. URL: http://news.nationalgeographic.com/news/2005/09/0921_050921_amazon_ant.html. Accessed on March 19, 2008.

Royal Society of Chemistry. "The chemistry of bees." Available online. URL: http://www.chemsoc.org/ExemplarChem/entries/2001/loveridge/index-page8.html. Accessed on March 19, 2008.

Schwarcz, Joe. *Radar, Hula Hoops, and Playful Pigs: 67 Digestible Commentaries on the Fascinating Chemistry of Everyday Life.* New York: Henry Holt & Co., 2002.

ScienceDaily. "Chlorine can react with sweat, urine at indoor swimming pools forming volatile disinfection byproducts." Available online. URL: http://www.sciencedaily.com/releases/2008/02/080219161946.htm. Accessed on March 19, 2008.

Senese, Fred. "The molecular basis of indicator color changes," Frostburg State University's Department of Chemistry Web site. Available online. URL: http://antoine.frostburg.edu/chem/senese/101/features/water2wine.shtml. Accessed on March 13, 2008.

Senese, Fred. "Why is nitroglycerin explosive?" Frostburg State University's Department of Chemistry Web site. Available online. URL: http://antoine.frostburg.edu/chem/senese/101/ redox/faq/nitroglycerin.shtml. Accessed on March 11, 2008.

Shakhashiri, Bassam. "Chemical of the week: phosphoric acid," University of Wisconsin-Madison Web site. Available online. URL: http://scifun.chem.wisc.edu/CHEMWEEK/PDF/ Phosphoric_Acid.pdf. Accessed on March 17, 2008.

Shakhashiri, Bassam. "Chemical of the week: sulfuric acid," University of Wisconsin-Madison Web site. Available online. URL: http://scifun.chem.wisc.edu/chemweek/Sulf&top/Sulf&Top. html. Accessed on March 17, 2008.

Smithsonian Center for Materials Research & Education. "Acid free tissue paper for textiles & costumes." Available online. URL: http://www.si.edu/MCI/english/learn_more/taking_care/ acidfree.html. Accessed on March 10, 2008.

Texas A&M University Department of Entomology. "Carpenter ant, Camponotus spp." Available online. URL: http:// urbanentomology.tamu.edu/ants/carpenter.cfm. Accessed on March 19, 2008.

U.S. Environmental Protection Agency. "Acid rain." Available online. URL: http://www.epa.gov/acidrain/index.html. Accessed on March 19, 2008.

VanCleave, Janice. "Is it acid or base? These colorful tests tell all!" *Instructor* (1990): 97–98.

Zaslow, Sandra. "Removing mineral deposits from household surfaces," North Carolina State University-Department of Biological and Agricultural Engineering Web site. Available online. URL: http://www.bae.ncsu.edu/programs/extension/publicat/ wqwm/he397.html. Accessed on March 17, 2008.

FURTHER READING

Baldwin, Carol. *Acids and Bases*. Austin, Tex.: Raintree Publishers, 2005.

Bardhan-Quallen, Sudipta. *Championship Science Fair Projects: 100 Sure-to-Win Experiments*. New York: Sterling Publishing, 2007.

Goss, Tim. *Venus*. Chicago: Heinemann Library, 2007.

Hewitt, Sally. *Everyday Chemicals*. Minneapolis, Minn.: Lerner Publishing Group, 2003.

Karpelenia, Jenny. *Acids and Bases*. Logan, Iowa: Perfection Learning, 2005.

Levine, Shar and Leslie Johnstone. *Kitchen Science*. New York: Sterling Publishing, 2005.

Moje, Steven. *Cool Chemistry: Great Experiments with Simple Stuff*. New York: Sterling Publishing, 2001.

Oxlade, Chris. *Acids and Bases*. Chicago: Heinemann Library, 2007.

Parks, Peggy. *Acid Rain*. Detroit, Mich: Gale Group, 2005.

Powell, Jillian. *Fats for a Healthy Body*. Chicago: Heinemann, 2003.

Walker, Denise. *Acids and Alkalis*. Mankato, Minn.: Black Rabbit Books, 2007.

Web Sites

Chem4Kids.com

http://www.chem4kids.com/files/react_acidbase.html

This Web site explains and provides example of many chemistry-related topics—matter, atoms, the periodic table, and chemical reactions, just to name a few.

EPA's Acid Rain Kid's Site

http://www.epa.gov/acidrain/education/site_kids/index.htm

The Environmental Protection Agency's Web site explains how acid rain forms, what it does to the environment, and ways we can all help reduce the presence of acid rain.

Home Experiments

http://scifun.chem.wisc.edu/HOMEEXPTS/HOMEEXPTS.html

This Web site provides a collection of science experiments you can do at home, including making a red cabbage pH indicator, removing tarnish from silver, and making things fizz and foam.

Jefferson Lab

http://education.jlab.org/indexpages/index.php

Jefferson Lab's Student Zone Web site contains an interactive periodic table, information about science laboratory summer internships, and online games and puzzles.

NOVA

http://www.pbs.org/wgbh/nova/

The NOVA Web site contains online videos and interactive articles explaining science topics from chemistry and physics to oceanography and nanotechnology.

PHOTO CREDITS

INDEX

ABOUT THE AUTHOR

KRISTI LEW is a former high school science teacher with degrees in biochemistry and genetics. After years in the classroom and cyto-genetics laboratories, she decided that she wanted to write full-time. She is the author of more than 20 nonfiction science books for students and teachers.